Robert Herrick

The Hesperides and Noble Numbers

Vol. I

Robert Herrick

The Hesperides and Noble Numbers
Vol. I

ISBN/EAN: 9783744711715

Printed in Europe, USA, Canada, Australia, Japan

Cover: Foto ©Andreas Hilbeck / pixelio.de

More available books at **www.hansebooks.com**

ROBERT HERRICK

THE HESPERIDES & NOBLE

NUMBERS : EDITED BY

ALFRED POLLARD

WITH A PREFACE BY

A. C. SWINBURNE

Vol. I.

REVISED EDITION

LONDON :

LAWRENCE & BULLEN, Ltd.,

16 Henrietta Street, W.C.

1898.

NEW YORK :

CHARLES SCRIBNER'S SONS,

153-157 Fifth Avenue.

1898.

EDITOR'S NOTE.

In this edition of Herrick quotation is for the first time facilitated by the poems being numbered according to their order in the original edition. This numbering has rendered it possible to print those Epigrams, which successive editors have joined in deploring, in a detachable Appendix, their place in the original being indicated by the numeration. It remains to be added that the footnotes in this edition are intended to explain, as unobtrusively as possible, difficulties of phrase or allusion which might conceivably hinder the understanding of Herrick's meaning. In the longer Notes at the end of each volume earlier versions of some important poems are printed from manuscripts at the British Museum, and an endeavour has been made to extend the list of Herrick's debts to classical sources, and to identify some of his friends who have hitherto escaped research. An editor is always apt to mention his predecessors rather for blame than praise, and I therefore take this opportunity of acknowledging my general indebtedness to the pioneer work of Mr. Hazlitt and Dr. Grosart, upon whose foundations all editors of Herrick must necessarily build.

ALFRED W. POLLARD.

PREFACE.

It is singular that the first great age of English
lyric poetry should have been also the one
great age of English dramatic poetry: but it is
hardly less singular that the lyric school should
have advanced as steadily as the dramatic
school declined from the promise of its dawn.
Born with Marlowe, it rose at once with
Shakespeare to heights inaccessible before and
since and for ever, to sink through bright gra-
dations of glorious decline to its final and
beautiful sunset in Shirley: but the lyrical
record that begins with the author of "Euphues" and "Endymion" grows fuller if not
brighter through a whole chain of constellations till it culminates in the crowning star of
Herrick. Shakespeare's last song, the exquisite
and magnificent overture to "The Two Noble
Kinsmen," is hardly so limpid in its flow, so
liquid in its melody, as the two great songs in
"Valentinian": but Herrick, our last poet of
that incomparable age or generation, has

matched them again and again.   As a creative
and inventive singer, he surpasses all his rivals
in quantity of good work; in quality of spon-
taneous instinct and melodious inspiration he
reminds us, by frequent and flawless evidence,
who above all others must beyond all doubt
have been his first master and his first model
in lyric poetry—the author of " The Passionate
Shepherd to his Love ".

The last of his line, he is and will probably
be always the first in rank and station of
English song-writers.   We have only to remember how rare it is to find a perfect song,
good to read and good to sing, combining the
merits of Coleridge and Shelley with the capa-
bilities of Tommy Moore and Haynes Bayly,
to appreciate the unique and unapproachable
excellence of Herrick.   The lyrist who wished
to be a butterfly, the lyrist who fled or flew to
a lone vale at the hour (whatever hour it may
be) "when stars are weeping," have left behind them such stuff as may be sung, but
certainly cannot be read and endured by any
one with an ear for verse.   The author of the
Ode on France and the author of the Ode to
the West Wind have left us hardly more than
a song a-piece which has been found fit for setting to music: and, lovely as they are, the
fame of their authors does not mainly depend

on the song of Glycine or the song of which
Leigh Hunt so justly and so critically said that
Beaumont and Fletcher never wrote anything
of the kind more lovely. Herrick, of course,
lives simply by virtue of his songs; his more
ambitious or pretentious lyrics are merely
magnified and prolonged and elaborated songs.
Elegy or litany, epicede or epithalamium, his
work is always a song-writer's; nothing more,
but nothing less, than the work of the greatest
song-writer—as surely as Shakespeare is the
greatest dramatist—ever born of English race.
The apparent or external variety of his versifi-
cation is, I should suppose, incomparable; but
by some happy tact or instinct he was too
naturally unambitious to attempt, like Jonson,
a flight in the wake of Pindar. He knew what
he could not do: a rare and invaluable gift.
Born a blackbird or a thrush, he did not take
himself (or try) to be a nightingale.

It has often been objected that he did mis-
take himself for a sacred poet : and it cannot be
denied that his sacred verse at its worst is as
offensive as his secular verse at its worst; nor
can it be denied that no severer sentence of
condemnation can be passed upon any poet's
work. But neither Herbert nor Crashaw could
have bettered such a divinely beautiful triplet
as this :—

" We see Him come, and know Him ours,
Who with His sunshine and His showers
Turns all the patient ground to flowers ".

That is worthy of Miss Rossetti herself : and praise of such work can go no higher.

But even such exquisite touches or tones of colour may be too often repeated in fainter shades or more glaring notes of assiduous and facile reiteration. The sturdy student who tackles his Herrick as a schoolboy is expected to tackle his Horace, in a spirit of pertinacious and stolid straightforwardness, will probably find himself before long so nauseated by the incessant inhalation of spices and flowers, con-diments and kisses, that if a musk-rat had run over the page it could hardly be less endurable to the physical than it is to the spiritual stomach. The fantastic and the brutal blem-ishes which deform and deface the loveliness of his incomparable genius are hardly so damaging to his fame as his general monotony of matter and of manner. It was doubtless in order to relieve this saccharine and " mellisonant " monotony that he thought fit to intersperse these interminable droppings of natural or artificial perfume with others of the rankest and most intolerable odour : but a diet of alter-nate sweetmeats and emetics is for the average of eaters and drinkers no less unpalatable than unwholesome. It is useless and thankless to enlarge on such faults or such defects, as it would be useless and senseless to ignore. But how to enlarge, to expatiate, to insist on the charm of Herrick at his best—a charm so incomparable and so inimitable that even English poetry can boast of nothing quite like it or worthy to be named after it—the most appreciative reader will be the slowest to affirm or imagine that he can conjecture. This, however, he will hardly fail to remark: that Herrick, like most if not all other lyric poets, is not best known by his best work. If we may judge by frequency of quotation or of reference, the ballad of the ride from Ghent to Aix is a far more popular, more generally admired and accredited specimen of Mr. Browning's work than "The Last Ride Together"—and "The Lost Leader" than "The Lost Mistress". Yet the superiority of the less-popular poem is in either case beyond all question or comparison: in depth and in glow of spirit and of harmony, in truth and charm of thought and word, undeniable and indescribable. No two men of genius were ever more unlike than the authors of "Paracelsus" and "Hesperides": and yet it is as true of Herrick as of Browning that his best is not always his best-known work. Everyone knows the song, "Gather ye rosebuds while ye

may"; few, I fear, by comparison, know the
yet sweeter and better song, "Ye have been
fresh and green". The general monotony of
style and motive which fatigues and irritates
his too-persevering reader is here and there
relieved by a change of key which anticipates
the note of a later and very different lyric
school. The brilliant simplicity and pointed
grace of the three stanzas to Œnone ("What
conscience, say, is it in thee") recall the lyrists
of the Restoration in their cleanlier and happier
mood. And in the very fine epigram headed by
the words "Devotion makes the Deity" he has
expressed for once a really high and deep
thought in words of really noble and severe
propriety. His "Mad Maid's Song," again, can
only be compared with Blake's; which has
more of passionate imagination, if less of pa-
thetic sincerity.

A. C. SWINBURNE.

LIFE OF HERRICK.

OF the lives of many poets we know too much; of some few too little. Lovers of Herrick are almost ideally fortunate. Just such a bare outline of his life has come down to us as is sufficient to explain the allusions in his poems, and, on the other hand, there is no temptation to substitute chatter about his relations with Julia and Dianeme for enjoyment of his delightful verse. The recital of the bare outline need detain us but a few minutes: only the least imaginative of readers will have any difficulty in filling it in from the poems themselves.

From early in the fourteenth century onwards we hear of the family of Eyrick or Herrick at Stretton, in Leicestershire. At the beginning of the sixteenth century we find a branch of it settled in Leicester itself, where John Eyrick, the poet's grandfather, was admitted a freeman in 1535, and afterwards acted as Mayor. This John's second son, Nicholas, migrated to

b

London, became a goldsmith in Wood Street, Cheapside, and, according to a licence issued by the Bishop of London, December 8, 1582, married Julian, daughter of William Stone, sister of Anne, wife of Sir Stephen Soame, Lord Mayor of London in 1598. The marriage was not unfruitful. A William* Herrick was baptized at St. Vedast's, Foster Lane, November 24, 1585; Martha, January 22, 1586; Mercy, December 22, 1586; Thomas, May 7, 1588; Nicholas, April 22, 1589; Anne, July 26, 1590; and Robert himself, August 24, 1591.

Fifteen months after the poet's birth, on November 7, 1592, Nicholas Herrick made his will, estimating his property as worth £3000, and devising it, as to one-third to his wife, and as to the other two-thirds to his children in equal shares. In the will he described himself as "of perfect memorye in sowle, but sicke in bodye". Two days after its execution he was buried, having died, not from disease, but from a fall from an upper window. His death had so much the appearance of self-destruction that £220 had to be paid to the High Almoner, Dr. Fletcher, Bishop

---

* A second William is said to have been born, posthumously, in "Harry Campion's house at Hampton," in 1593.

of Bristol, in satisfaction of his official claim to the goods and chattels of suicides. Herrick's biographers have not failed to vituperate the Bishop for his avarice, but dues allowed by law are hardly to be abandoned because a baby of fifteen months is destined to become a brilliant poet, and no other exceptional circumstances are alleged. The estate of Nicholas Herrick could the better afford the fine inasmuch as it realized £2000 more than was expected.

By the will Robert and William Herrick were appointed "overseers," or trustees for the children. The former was the poet's god-father, and in his will of 1617 left him £5. To William Herrick, then recently knighted for his services as goldsmith, jeweller, and moneylender to James I., the young Robert was apprenticed for ten years, September 25, 1607. An allusion to "beloved Westminster," in his *Tears to Thamesis*, has been taken to refer to Westminster school, and alleged as proof that he was educated there. Dr. Grosart even presses the mention of Richmond, Kingston, and Hampton Court to support a conjecture that Herrick may have travelled up and down to school from Hampton. If so, one wonders what his headmaster had to say to the "soft-smooth virgins, for our chaste disport"

by whom he was accompanied. But the references in the poem are surely to his courtier-
life in London, and after his father's death
the apprenticeship to his uncle in 1607 is
the first fact in his life of which we can be
sure.

In 1607, Herrick was fifteen, and, even
if we conjecture that he may have been
allowed to remain at school some little time
after his apprenticeship nominally began, he
must have served his uncle for five or six
years. Sir William had himself been bound
apprentice in a similar way to the poet's
father, and we have no evidence that he
exacted any premium. At any rate, when in
1614, his nephew, then of age, desired to leave
the business and go to Cambridge, the ten
years' apprenticeship did not stand in his way,
and he entered as a Fellow Commoner at St.
John's. His uncle plainly still managed his
affairs, for an amusing series of fourteen letters
has been preserved at Beaumanor, until lately
the seat of Sir William's descendants, in which
the poet asks sometimes for payment of a
quarterly stipend of £10, sometimes for a
formal loan, sometimes for the help of his
avuncular Mæcenas. It seems a fair inference
from this variety of requests that, since Herrick's share of his father's property could

hardly have yielded a yearly income of £40, he was allowed to draw on his capital for this sum, but that his uncle and Lady Herrick occasionally made him small presents, which may account for his tone of dependence.

The quarterly stipend was paid through various booksellers, but irregularly, so that the poor poet was frequently reduced to great straits, though £40 a-year (£200 of our money) was no bad allowance. After two years he migrated from St. John's to Trinity Hall, to study law and curtail his expenses. He took his Bachelor's degree from there in January, 1617, and his Master's in 1620. The fourteen letters show that he had prepared himself for University life by cultivating a very florid prose style which frequently runs into decasyllabics, perhaps a result of a study of the dramatists. Sir William Herrick is sometimes addressed in them as his most "careful" uncle, but at the time of his migration the poet speaks of his "ebbing estate," and as late as 1629 he was still £10 16s. 9d. in debt to the College Steward. We can thus hardly imagine that he was possessed of any considerable private income when he returned to London, to live practically on his wits, and a study of his poems suggests that, the influence of the careful uncle removed, whatever capital he possessed was soon likely

to vanish.*   His verses to the Earl of Pembroke, to Endymion Porter and to others, show
that he was glad of " pay " as well as " praise,"
but the system of patronage brought no dis-
credit with it, and though the absence of any
poetical mention of his uncle suggests that the
rich goldsmith was not well-pleased with his
nephew, with the rest of his well-to-do relations
Herrick seems to have remained on excellent
terms.

Besides patrons, such as Pembroke, Westmoreland, Newark, Buckingham, Herrick had
less distinguished friends at Court, Edward
Norgate, Jack Crofts and others.   He composed the words for two New Year anthems
which were set to music by Henry Lawes, and
he was probably personally known both to the
King and Queen.   Outside the Court he
reckoned himself one of Ben Jonson's dis-
ciples, " Sons of Ben " as they were called,
had friends at the Inns of Court, knew the
organist of Westminster Abbey and his pretty
daughters, and had every temptation to live an
amusing and expensive life.   His poems were
handed about in manuscript after the fashion

---

* Yet in his *Farewell to Poetry* he distinctly says :—

" I've more to bear my charge than way to go " ;
the line, however, is a translation from his favourite
Seneca, Ep. 77.

of the time, and wherever music and poetry were loved he was sure to be a welcome guest.

Mr. Hazlitt's conjecture that Herrick at this time may have held some small post in the Chapel at Whitehall is not unreasonable, but at what date he took Holy Orders is not known. In 1627 he obtained the post of chaplain to the unlucky expedition to the Isle of Rhé, and two years later (September 30, 1629) he was presented by the King to the Vicarage of Dean Prior, in Devonshire, which the promotion of its previous incumbent, Dr. Potter, to the Bishopric of Carlisle, had left in the royal gift. The annual value of the living was only £50 (£250 present value), no great prize, but the poem entitled *Mr. Robert Hericke : his farwell unto Poetrie* (not printed in *Hesperides*, but extant in more than one manuscript version) shows that the poet was not unaware of the responsibilities of his profession. " But unto me," he says to his Muse :

'' But unto me be only hoarse, since now
  (Heaven and my soul bear record of my vow)
  I my desires screw from thee and direct
  Them and my thoughts to that sublime respect
  And conscience unto priesthood. 'Tis not need
  (The scarecrow unto mankind) that doth breed
  Wiser conclusions in me, since I know
  I've more to bear my charge than way to go ;

Or had I not, I'd stop the spreading itch
Of craving more : so in conceit be rich ;
But 'tis the God of nature who intends
And shapes my function for more glorious ends."

Perhaps it was at this time too that Herrick wrote his *Farewell to Sack*, and although he returned both to sack and to poetry we should be wrong in imagining him as a "blind mouth," using his office merely as a means of gain. He celebrated the births of Charles II and his brother in verse, perhaps with an eye to future royal favours, but no more than Chaucer's good parson does he seem to have "run to London unto Seynte Poules" in search of the seventeenth century equivalent for a chauntry, and many of his poems show him living the life of a con-tented country clergyman, sharing the contents of bin and cruse with his poor parishioners, and jotting down sermon-notes in verse.

The great majority of Herrick's poems cannot be dated, and it is idle to enquire which were written before his ordination and which after-wards. His conception of religion was medieval in its sensuousness, and he probably repeated the stages of sin, repentance and renewed assur-ance with some facility. He lived with an old servant, Prudence Baldwin, the "Prew" of many of his poems ; kept a spaniel named Tracy, and, so says tradition, a tame pig.

When his parishioners annoyed him he seems
to have comforted himself with epigrams on
them ; when they slumbered during one of his
sermons the manuscript was suddenly hurled
at them with a curse for their inattention.

In the same year that Herrick was appointed
to his country vicarage his mother died while
living with her daughter, Mercy, the poet's
dearest sister (see 818), then for some time
married to John Wingfield of Brantham in
Suffolk (see 590), by whom she had three sons
and a daughter, also called Mercy. His eldest
brother, Thomas, had been placed with a Mr.
Massam, a merchant, but as early as 1610 had
retired to live a country life in Leicestershire
(see 106). He appears to have married a wife
named Elizabeth, whose loss Herrick laments
(see 72). Nicholas, the next brother was more
adventurous. He had become a merchant
trading to the Levant, and in this capacity had
visited the Holy Land (see 1100). To his wife
Susanna, daughter of William Salter, Herrick
addresses two poems (522 and 977). There
were three sons and four daughters in this
family, and Herrick wrote a poem to one of the
daughters, Bridget (562), and an elegy on
another, Elizabeth (376). When Mrs. Herrick died the bulk of her property was left to
the Wingfields, but William Herrick received a

legacy of £100, with ten pounds apiece to his
two children, and a ring of twenty shillings to
his wife. Nicholas and Robert were only left
twenty-shilling rings, and the administration of
the will was entrusted to William Herrick and
the Wingfields. The will may have been the
result of a family arrangement, and we have no
reason to believe that the unequal division gave
rise to any ill-feeling. Herrick's address to
" his dying brother, Master William Herrick "
(186), shows abundant affection, and there is
every reason to believe that it was addressed
to the William who administered to Mrs. Herrick's will.

While little nephews and nieces were springing up around him, Herrick remained unmarried,
and frequently congratulates himself on his
freedom from the yoke matrimonial. He ima-
gined how he would bid farewell to his wife,
if he had one (465), and wrote magnificent
epithalamia for his friends, but lived and died
a bachelor. When first civil troubles and then
civil war cast a shadow over the land, it is not
very easy to say how he viewed the contending
parties. He was devoted to Charles and Henrietta Maria and the young Prince of Wales,
and rejoiced at every Royalist success. Many
also of his poems breathe the spirit of un-
questioning loyalty, but in others he is less

certain of kingly wisdom. Something, however, must be allowed for his evident habit of
versifying any phrase or epigram which im-
pressed him, and not all his poems need be
regarded as expressions of his personal opi-
nions. But with whatever doubts his loyalty
was qualified, it was sufficiently obvious to
procure his ejection from his living in 1648 ;
and, making the best of his loss, he bade farewell to Dean Prior, shook the dust of "loathed
Devonshire " off his feet, and returned gaily to
London, where he appears to have discarded
his clerical habit and to have been made abun-
dantly welcome by his friends.

Free from the cares of his incumbency, and
free also from the restraints it imposed,
Herrick's thoughts turned to the publication
of his poems. As we have said, in his old
Court-days these had found some circulation
in manuscript, and in 1635 one of his fairy
poems was printed, probably without his
leave (see Appendix). In 1639 his poem (575)
*The Apparition of his Mistress calling him
to Elysium* was licensed at Stationers' Hall
under the title of *His Mistress' Shade*, and it
was included the next year in an edition of
Shakespeare's Poems (see Notes). On April
29, 1640, "The severall poems written by
Master Robert Herrick," were entered as to be

published by Andrew Crook, but no trace of
such a volume has been discovered, and it was
only in 1648 that *Hesperides* at length appeared.
Two years later upwards of eighty of the
poems in it were printed in the 1650 edition of
Witt's Recreations, but a small number of these
show considerable variations from the *Hesperides* versions, and it is probable that they were
printed from the poet's manuscript. Compilers
of other miscellanies and song books laid Herrick under contribution, but, with the one
exception of his contribution to the *Lacrymæ
Musarum* in 1649, no fresh production of his
pen has been preserved, and we know nothing
further of his life save that he returned to
Dean Prior after the Restoration (August 24,
1662), and that according to the parish register
"Robert Herrick, Vicker, was buried ye 15th
day October, 1674."

ALFRED W. POLLARD

NOTE TO SECOND EDITION.

IN this edition some trifling errors, which had crept into the text and the numeration of the poems, have been corrected, and many fresh illustrations of Herrick's reading added in the notes, which have elsewhere been slightly compressed to make room for them. Almost all of the new notes have been supplied from the manuscript collections of a veteran student of Herrick who placed himself in correspondence with me after the publication of my first edition. To my great regret I am not allowed to make my acknowledgments to him by name.

A. W. P.

HESPERIDES:

OR,

THE WORKS

BOTH

HUMANE & DIVINE

OF

ROBERT HERRICK *Esq.*

OVID.

Effugient avidos Carmina nostra Rogos.

L O N D O N,

Printed for *John Williams,* and *Francis Eglesfield.*
and are to be sold by *Tho: Hunt,* Book-seller
in *Exon.* 1648.

TO THE

Most Illustrious and Most Hopeful Prince.

CHARLES,

PRINCE OF WALES.

WELL may my book come forth like public day.
When such a light as you are leads the way,
Who are my work's creator, and alone
The flame of it, and the expansion.
And look how all those heavenly lamps acquire
Light from the sun, that inexhausted fire,
So all my morn and evening stars from you
Have their existence, and their influence too.
Full is my book of glories; but all these
By you become immortal substances.

HESPERIDES.

I. THE ARGUMENT OF HIS BOOK.

I sing of brooks, of blossoms, birds and bowers,
Of April, May, of June and July-flowers ;
I sing of May-poles, hock-carts, wassails, wakes,
Of bridegrooms, brides and of their bridal cakes;
I write of youth, of love, and have access
By these to sing of cleanly wantonness ;
I sing of dews, of rains, and piece by piece
Of balm, of oil, of spice and ambergris ;
I sing of times trans-shifting, and I write
How roses first came red and lilies white ;
I write of groves, of twilights, and I sing
The Court of Mab, and of the Fairy King ;
I write of hell ; I sing (and ever shall)
Of heaven, and hope to have it after all.

Hock-cart, the last cart from the harvest-field.
Wakes, village festivals, properly on the dedication-
day of a church.
Ambergris, 'grey amber,' much used in perfumery.

2. TO HIS MUSE.

WHITHER, mad maiden, wilt thou roam?
Far safer 'twere to stay at home,
Where thou mayst sit and piping please
The poor and private cottages,
Since cotes and hamlets best agree
With this thy meaner minstrelsy.
There with the reed thou mayst express
The shepherd's fleecy happiness,
And with thy eclogues intermix
Some smooth and harmless bucolics.
There on a hillock thou mayst sing
Unto a handsome shepherdling,
Or to a girl, that keeps the neat,
With breath more sweet than violet.
There, there, perhaps, such lines as these
May take the simple villages;
But for the court, the country wit
Is despicable unto it.
Stay, then, at home, and do not go
Or fly abroad to seek for woe.
Contempts in courts and cities dwell,
No critic haunts the poor man's cell,
Where thou mayst hear thine own lines read
By no one tongue there censured.
That man's unwise will search for ill,
And may prevent it, sitting still.

3. TO HIS BOOK.

WHILE thou didst keep thy candour undefil'd,
Dearly I lov'd thee as my first-born child,
' But when I saw thee wantonly to roam
From house to house, and never stay at home,
I brake my bonds of love, and bade thee go,
Regardless whether well thou sped'st or no.
On with thy fortunes then, whate'er they be:
If good, I'll smile; if bad, I'll sigh for thee.

4. ANOTHER.

To read my book the virgin shy
May blush while Brutus standeth by,
But when he's gone, read through what's writ,
And never stain a cheek ior it.

7. TO HIS BOOK.

COME thou not near those men who are like bread
O'er-leaven'd, or like cheese o'er-renneted.

8. WHEN HE WOULD HAVE HIS VERSES READ.

IN sober mornings, do not thou rehearse
The holy incantation of a verse;
But when that men have both well drunk and fed,
Let my enchantments then be sung or read.

Brutus, see Martial, xi. 16, quoted in Note at the end
of the volume

When laurel spirts i'th' fire, and when the hearth
Smiles to itself, and gilds the roof with mirth ;
When up the thyrse * is rais'd, and when the sound
Of sacred orgies † flies, a round, a round.
When the rose reigns, and locks with ointments shine,
Let rigid Cato read these lines of mine.

9. UPON JULIA'S RECOVERY.

DROOP, droop no more, or hang the head,
Ye roses almost withered ;
Now strength and newer purple get,
Each here declining violet.
O primroses! let this day be
A resurrection unto ye ;
And to all flowers ally'd in blood,
Or sworn to that sweet sisterhood :
For health on Julia's cheek hath shed
Claret and cream commingled ;
And those her lips do now appear
As beams of coral, but more clear.

10. TO SILVIA TO WED.

LET us, though late, at last, my Silvia, wed,
And loving lie in one devoted bed.

* " A javelin twined with ivy " (Note in the original
edition).
† " Songs to Bacchus " (Note in the original edition.)
Round, a rustic dance.
Cato, see Martial, x. 17, quoted in Note.
Beams, perhaps here = branches : but cp. 440.

Thy watch may stand, my minutes fly post-haste;
No sound calls back the year that once is past.
Then, sweetest Silvia, let's no longer stay;
True love, we know, precipitates delay.
Away with doubts, all scruples hence remove;
No man at one time can be wise and love.

II. THE PARLIAMENT OF ROSES TO JULIA.

I DREAMT the roses one time went
To meet and sit in parliament;
The place for these, and for the rest
Of flowers, was thy spotless breast,
Over the which a state was drawn
Of tiffanie or cobweb lawn.
Then in that parly all those powers
Voted the rose the queen of flowers;
But so as that herself should be
The maid of honour unto thee.

12. NO BASHFULNESS IN BEGGING.

To get thine ends, lay bashfulness aside;
Who fears to ask doth teach to be deny'd.

State, a canopy.   *Tiffanie*, gauze.
    Parly, a parliament.

13. THE FROZEN HEART.

I FREEZE, I freeze, and nothing dwells
In me but snow and icicles.
For pity's sake, give your advice,
To melt this snow and thaw this ice.
I'll drink down flames; but if so be
Nothing but love can supple me,
I'll rather keep this frost and snow
Than to be thaw'd or heated so.

14. TO PERILLA.

AH, my Perilla! dost thou grieve to see
Me, day by day, to steal away from thee?
Age calls me hence, and my grey hairs bid come,
And haste away to mine eternal home;
'Twill not be long, Perilla, after this,
That I must give thee the supremest kiss.
Dead when I am, first cast in salt, and bring
Part of the cream from that religious spring;
With which, Perilla, wash my hands and feet;
That done, then wind me in that very sheet
Which wrapt thy smooth limbs when thou didst
    implore
The gods' protection but the night before.
Follow me weeping to my turf, and there
Let fall a primrose, and with it a tear:
Then, lastly, let some weekly-strewings be
Devoted to the memory of me:
Then shall my ghost not walk about, but keep
Still in the cool and silent shades of sleep.

Weekly strewings, i.e., of flowers on his grave.
First cast in salt, cp. 769.

15. A SONG TO THE MASKERS.

COME down and dance ye in the toil
 Of pleasures to a heat;
But if to moisture, let the oil
 Of roses be your sweat.

Not only to yourselves assume
 These sweets, but let them fly
From this to that, and so perfume
 E'en all the standers by;

As goddess Isis, when she went
 Or glided through the street,
Made all that touched her, with her scent,
 And whom she touched, turn sweet.

16. TO PERENNA.

WHEN I thy parts run o'er, I can't espy
In any one the least indecency;
But every line and limb diffused thence
A fair and unfamiliar excellence:
So that the more I look the more I prove
There's still more cause why I the more should love.

17. TREASON.

THE seeds of treason choke up as they spring:
He acts the crime that gives it cherishing.

Indecency, uncomeliness.

18. TWO THINGS ODIOUS.

Two of a thousand things are disallow'd :
A lying rich man, and a poor man proud.

19. TO HIS MISTRESSES.

HELP me! help me! now I call
To my pretty witchcrafts all ;
Old I am, and cannot do
That I was accustomed to.
Bring your magics, spells, and charms,
To enflesh my thighs and arms.
Is there no way to beget
In my limbs their former heat ?
Æson had, as poets feign,
Baths that made him young again :
Find that medicine, if you can,
For your dry decrepit man
Who would fain his strength renew,
Were it but to pleasure you.

20. THE WOUNDED HEART.

COME bring your sampler, and with art
  Draw in't a wounded heart
  And dropping here and there :
Not that I think that any dart
  Can make yours bleed a tear,
  Or pierce it anywhere ;
Yet do it to this end : that I
  May by

Æson, rejuvenated by Medea ; see Ovid, Met. vii.

This secret see,
Though you can make
That heart to bleed, yours ne'er will ache
For me.

21. NO LOATHSOMENESS IN LOVE.

WHAT I fancy I approve,
No dislike there is in love.
Be my mistress short or tall,
And distorted therewithal :
Be she likewise one of those
That an acre hath of nose :
Be her forehead and her eyes
Full of incongruities :
Be her cheeks so shallow too
As to show her tongue wag through ;
Be her lips ill hung or set,
And her grinders black as jet :
Has she thin hair, hath she none,
She's to me a paragon.

22. TO ANTHEA.

IF, dear Anthea, my hard fate it be
To live some few sad hours after thee,
Thy sacred corse with odours I will burn,
And with my laurel crown thy golden urn.
Then holding up there such religious things
As were, time past, thy holy filletings,
Near to thy reverend pitcher I will fall
Down dead for grief, and end my woes withal :
So three in one small plat of ground shall lie—
Anthea, Herrick, and his poetry.

23. THE WEEPING CHERRY.

I SAW a cherry weep, and why?
　　Why wept it? but for shame
Because my Julia's lip was by,
　　And did out-red the same.
But, pretty fondling, let not fall
　　A tear at all for that:
Which rubies, corals, scarlets, all
　　For tincture wonder at.

24. SOFT MUSIC.

THE mellow touch of music most doth wound
The soul when it doth rather sigh than sound.

25. THE DIFFERENCE BETWIXT KINGS AND SUBJECTS.

'TWIXT kings and subjects there's this mighty odds:
Subjects are taught by men; kings by the gods.

26. HIS ANSWER TO A QUESTION.

SOME would know
　　Why I so
Long still do tarry,
　　And ask why
　　Here that I
Live and not marry.
　　Thus I those
　　Do oppose:
What man would be here
　　Slave to thrall,
　　If at all
He could live free here?

27. UPON JULIA'S FALL.

JULIA was careless, and withal
She rather took than got a fall,
The wanton ambler chanc'd to see
Part of her legs' sincerity:
And ravish'd thus, it came to pass,
The nag (like to the prophet's ass)
Began to speak, and would have been
A-telling what rare sights he'd seen :
And had told all; but did refrain
Because his tongue was tied again.

28. EXPENSES EXHAUST.

LIVE with a thrifty, not a needy fate ;
Small shots paid often waste a vast estate.

29. LOVE, WHAT IT IS.

LOVE is a circle that doth restless move
In the same sweet eternity of love.

30. PRESENCE AND ABSENCE.

WHEN what is lov'd is present, love doth spring ;
But being absent, love lies languishing.

Shots, debts.

31. NO SPOUSE BUT A SISTER.

A BACHELOR I will
Live as I have liv'd still,
And never take a wife
To crucify my life ;
But this I'll tell ye too,
What now I mean to do:
A sister (in the stead
Of wife) about I'll lead ;
Which I will keep embrac'd,
And kiss, but yet be chaste.

32. THE POMANDER BRACELET.

To me my Julia lately sent
A bracelet richly redolent:
The beads I kissed, but most lov'd her
That did perfume the pomander.

33. THE SHOE-TYING.

ANTHEA bade me tie her shoe ;
I did ; and kissed the instep too:
And would have kissed unto her knee,
Had not her blush rebuked me.

Pomander, a ball of scent.

34. THE CARCANET.

INSTEAD of orient pearls,of jet
I sent my love a carcanet;
About her spotless neck she knit
The lace, to honour me or it:
Then think how rapt was I to see
My jet t'enthral such ivory.

35. HIS SAILING FROM JULIA.

WHEN that day comes, whose evening says I'm gone
Unto that watery desolation,
Devoutly to thy closet-gods then pray
That my wing'd ship may meet no remora.
Those deities which circum-walk the seas,
And look upon our dreadful passages,
Will from all dangers re-deliver me
For one drink-offering poured out by thee.
Mercy and truth live with thee! and forbear
(In my short absence) to unsluice a tear;
But yet for love's sake let thy lips do this,
Give my dead picture one engendering kiss:
Work that to life, and let me ever dwell
In thy remembrance, Julia. So farewell.

Carcanet, necklace.
Lace, any kind of girdle; used here for the necklace.
Closet-gods, the Roman Lares.
Remora, the sea Lamprey or suckstone, believed to
check the course of ships by clinging to their keels.

36. HOW THE WALL-FLOWER CAME FIRST, AND WHY SO CALLED.

WHY this flower is now call'd so,
List, sweet maids, and you shall know.
Understand, this firstling was
Once a brisk and bonnie lass,
Kept as close as Danaë was :
Who a sprightly springall lov'd,
And to have it fully prov'd,
Up she got upon a wall,
Tempting down to slide withal :
But the silken twist untied,
So she fell, and, bruis'd, she died.
Love, in pity of the deed,
And her loving-luckless speed,
Turn'd her to this plant we call
Now *the flower of the wall.*

37. WHY FLOWERS CHANGE COLOUR.

THESE fresh beauties (we can prove)
Once were virgins sick of love.
Turn'd to flowers,—still in some
Colours go and colours come.

38. TO HIS MISTRESS OBJECTING TO HIM NEITHER TOYING OR TALKING.

YOU say I love not, 'cause I do not play
Still with your curls, and kiss the time away.

Tempting, trying.

You blame me too, because I can't devise
Some sport to please those babies in your eyes :
By love's religion, I must here confess it,
The most I love when I the least express it.
Small griefs find tongues : full casks are ever found
To give (if any, yet) but little sound.
Deep waters noiseless are ; and this we know,
That chiding streams betray small depth below.
So, when love speechless is, she doth express
A depth in love and that depth bottomless.
Now, since my love is tongueless, know me such
Who speak but little 'cause I love so much.

39. UPON THE LOSS OF HIS MISTRESSES.

I HAVE lost, and lately, these
Many dainty mistresses :
Stately Julia, prime of all :
Sappho next, a principal :
Smooth Anthea for a skin
White, and heaven-like crystalline :
Sweet Electra, and the choice
Myrrha for the lute and voice :
Next Corinna, for her wit,
And the graceful use of it :
With Perilla : all are gone ;
Only Herrick's left alone
For to number sorrow by
Their departures hence, and die.

Babies in your eyes, see Note.
2

40. THE DREAM.

METHOUGHT last night Love in an anger came
And brought a rod, so whipt me with the same ;
Myrtle the twigs were, merely to imply
Love strikes, but 'tis with gentle cruelty.
Patient I was : Love pitiful grew then
And strok'd the stripes, and I was whole again.
Thus, like a bee, Love gentle still doth bring
Honey to salve where he before did sting.

42. TO LOVE.

I'M free from thee ; and thou no more shalt hear
My puling pipe to beat against thine ear.
Farewell my shackles, though of pearl they be;
Such precious thraldom ne'er shall fetter me.
He loves his bonds who, when the first are broke,
Submits his neck unto a second yoke.

43. ON HIMSELF.

YOUNG I was, but now am old,
But I am not yet grown cold;
I can play, and I can twine
'Bout a virgin like a vine:
In her lap too I can lie
Melting, and in fancy die;
And return to life if she
Claps my cheek, or kisseth me:
Thus, and thus it now appears
That our love outlasts our years.

44. LOVE'S PLAY AT PUSH-PIN.

LOVE and myself, believe me, on a day
At childish push-pin, for our sport, did play;
I put, he pushed, and, heedless of my skin,
Love pricked my finger with a golden pin;
Since which it festers so that I can prove
'Twas but a trick to poison me with love:
Little the wound was, greater was the smart,
The finger bled, but burnt was all my heart.

45. THE ROSARY

ONE ask'd me where the roses grew:
 I bade him not go seek,
But forthwith bade my Julia show
 A bud in either cheek.

46. UPON CUPID.

OLD wives have often told how they
Saw Cupid bitten by a flea;
And thereupon, in tears half drown'd,
He cried aloud: Help, help the wound!
He wept, he sobb'd, he call'd to some
To bring him lint and balsamum,
To make a tent, and put it in
Where the stiletto pierced the skin;
Which, being done, the fretful pain
Assuaged, and he was well again.

Push-pin, a game in which pins are pushed with an
endeavour to cross them.
Tent, a roll of lint for probing wounds.

47. THE PARCÆ ; OR, THREE DAINTY DESTINIES : THE ARMILLET.

THREE lovely sisters working were,
  As they were closely set,
Of soft and dainty maidenhair
  A curious armillet.
I, smiling, asked them what they did,
  Fair Destinies all three,
Who told me they had drawn a thread
  Of life, and 'twas for me.
They show'd me then how fine 'twas spun,
  And I reply'd thereto,—
" I care not now how soon 'tis done,
  Or cut, if cut by you ".

48. SORROWS SUCCEED.

WHEN one is past, another care we have :
Thus woe succeeds a woe, as wave a wave.

49. CHERRY-PIT.

JULIA and I did lately sit
Playing for sport at cherry-pit :
She threw ; I cast ; and, having thrown,
I got the pit, and she the stone.

50. TO ROBIN REDBREAST.

LAID out for dead, let thy last kindness be
With leaves and moss-work for to cover me :

Cherry-pit, a game in which cherry-stones were
pitched into a small hole.

And while the wood-nymphs my cold corpse inter,
Sing thou my dirge, sweet-warbling chorister !
For epitaph, in foliage, next write this :
Here, here the tomb of Robin Herrick is.

51. DISCONTENTS IN DEVON.

MORE discontents I never had
    Since I was born than here,
Where I have been, and still am sad,
    In this dull Devonshire ;
Yet, justly too, I must confess
    I ne'er invented such
Ennobled numbers for the press,
    Than where I loathed so much.

52. TO HIS PATERNAL COUNTRY.

O EARTH ! earth ! earth ! hear thou my voice, and be
Loving and gentle for to cover me :
Banish'd from thee I live, ne'er to return,
Unless thou giv'st my small remains an urn.

53. CHERRY-RIPE.

CHERRY-RIPE, ripe, ripe, I cry,
    Full and fair ones; come and buy.
If so be you ask me where
    They do grow, I answer : There,
Where my Julia's lips do smile ;
    There's the land, or cherry-isle,
Whose plantations fully show
    All the year where cherries grow.

54. TO HIS MISTRESSES.

Put on your silks, and piece by piece
Give them the scent of ambergris ;
And for your breaths, too, let them smell
Ambrosia-like, or nectarel ;
While other gums their sweets perspire,
By your own jewels set on fire.

55. TO ANTHEA.

Now is the time, when all the lights wax dim ;
And thou, Anthea, must withdraw from him
Who was thy servant.   Dearest, bury me
Under that Holy-oak or Gospel-tree,
Where, though thou see'st not, thou may'st think upon
Me, when thou yearly go'st procession ;
Or, for mine honour, lay me in that tomb
In which thy sacred relics shall have room.
For my embalming, sweetest, there will be
No spices wanting when I'm laid by thee.

56. THE VISION TO ELECTRA.

I dreamed we both were in a bed
Of roses, almost smothered :
The warmth and sweetness had me there
Made lovingly familiar,
But that I heard thy sweet breath say,
Faults done by night will blush by day.

Holy oak, the oak under which the minister read the
Gospel in the procession round the parish bounds in
Rogation week.

I kissed thee, panting, and, I call
Night to the record! that was all.
But, ah! if empty dreams so please,
Love give me more such nights as these.

57. DREAMS.

HERE we are all by day; by night we're hurl'd
By dreams, each one into a sev'ral world.

58. AMBITION.

IN man ambition is the common'st thing;
Each one by nature loves to be a king.

59. HIS REQUEST TO JULIA.

JULIA, if I chance to die
Ere I print my poetry,
I most humbly thee desire
To commit it to the fire:
Better 'twere my book were dead
Than to live not perfected.

60. MONEY GETS THE MASTERY.

FIGHT thou with shafts of silver and o'ercome,
When no force else can get the masterdom.

61. THE SCARE-FIRE.

WATER, water I desire,
Here's a house of flesh on fire;
Ope the fountains and the springs,
And come all to bucketings:
What ye cannot quench pull down;
Spoil a house to save a town:
Better 'tis that one should fall,
Than by one to hazard all.

Scare-fire, fire-alarm.

62. UPON SILVIA, A MISTRESS.

WHEN some shall say, Fair once my Silvia was,
Thou wilt complain, False now's thy looking-glass,
Which renders that quite tarnished which was green,
And priceless now what peerless once had been.
Upon thy form more wrinkles yet will fall,
And, coming down, shall make no noise at all.

63. CHEERFULNESS IN CHARITY; OR, THE SWEET SACRIFICE.

'TIS not a thousand bullocks' thighs
Can please those heav'nly deities,
If the vower don't express
In his offering cheerfulness.

65. SWEETNESS IN SACRIFICE.

'TIS not greatness they require
To be offer'd up by fire;
But 'tis sweetness that doth please
Those *Eternal Essences.*

66. STEAM IN SACRIFICE.

IF meat the gods give, I the steam
High-towering will devote to them,
Whose easy natures like it well,
If we the roast have, they the smell.

Priceless, valueless

67. UPON JULIA'S VOICE.

So smooth, so sweet, so silv'ry is thy voice,
As, could they hear, the damn'd would make no noise,
But listen to thee, walking in thy chamber,
Melting melodious words to lutes of amber.

68. AGAIN.

WHEN I thy singing next shall hear,
I'll wish I might turn all to ear
To drink in notes and numbers such
As blessed souls can't hear too much;
Then melted down, there let me lie
Entranc'd and lost confusedly,
And, by thy music stricken mute,
Die and be turn'd into a lute.

69. ALL THINGS DECAY AND DIE.

All things decay with time : the forest sees
The growth and downfall of her aged trees;
That timber tall, which threescore lusters stood
The proud dictator of the state-like wood,—
I mean (the sovereign of all plants) the oak,—
Droops, dies, and falls without the cleaver's stroke.

Amber, used here merely for any rich material : cp.
" Treading on amber with their silver feet ".
Lusters, the Roman reckoning of five years.

70. THE SUCCESSION OF THE FOUR SWEET MONTHS.

FIRST, April, she with mellow showers
Opens the way for early flowers;
Then after her comes smiling May,
In a more rich and sweet array;
Next enters June, and brings us more
Gems than those two that went before:
Then (lastly) July comes, and she
More wealth brings in than all those three.

71. NO SHIPWRECK OF VIRTUE. TO A FRIEND.

THOU sail'st with others in this Argus here;
Nor wreck or bulging thou hast cause to fear;
But trust to this, my noble passenger;
Who swims with virtue, he shall still be sure
(Ulysses-like) all tempests to endure,
And 'midst a thousand gulfs to be secure.

72. UPON HIS SISTER-IN-LAW, MISTRESS ELIZABETH HERRICK.

FIRST, for effusions due unto the dead,
My solemn vows have here accomplished:
Next, how I love thee, that my grief must tell,
Wherein thou liv'st for ever.   Dear, farewell.

Bulging, leaking.
Effusions, drink-offerings.

73. OF LOVE. A SONNET.

How love came in I do not know,
Whether by the eye, or ear, or no ;
Or whether with the soul it came
(At first) infused with the same ;
Whether in part 'tis here or there,
Or, like the soul, whole everywhere,
This troubles me : but I as well
As any other this can tell :
That when from hence she does depart
The outlet then is from the heart.

74. TO ANTHEA.

AH, my Anthea! Must my heart still break ?
(*Love makes me write, what shame forbids to speak.*)
Give me a kiss, and to that kiss a score ;
Then to that twenty add a hundred more :
A thousand to that hundred : so kiss on,
To make that thousand up a million.
Treble that million, and when that is done
Let's kiss afresh, as when we first begun.
But yet, though love likes well such scenes as these,
There is an act that will more fully please :
Kissing and glancing, soothing, all make way
But to the acting of this private play :
Name it I would ; but, being blushing red,
The rest I'll speak when we meet both in bed.

75. THE ROCK OF RUBIES, AND THE QUARRY OF PEARLS.

SOME ask'd me where the rubies grew,
   And nothing I did say:
But with my finger pointed to
   The lips of Julia.
Some ask'd how pearls did grow, and where;
   Then spoke I to my girl,
To part her lips, and show'd them there
   The quarrelets of Pearl.

76. CONFORMITY.

CONFORMITY was ever known
A foe to dissolution:
Nor can we that a ruin call,
Whose crack gives crushing unto all.

77. TO THE KING, UPON HIS COMING WITH HIS ARMY INTO THE WEST.

WELCOME, most welcome to our vows and us,
Most great and universal genius!
The drooping West, which hitherto has stood
As one in long-lamented widowhood,
Looks like a bride now, or a bed of flowers
Newly refresh'd both by the sun and showers.
War, which before was horrid, now appears
Lovely in you, brave prince of cavaliers!
A deal of courage in each bosom springs
By your access, O you the best of kings!
Ride on with all white omens; so that where
Your standard's up, we fix a conquest there.

Quarrelets, little squares.

78. UPON ROSES.

UNDER a lawn, than skies more clear,
Some ruffled roses nestling were :
And, snugging there, they seem'd to lie
As in a flowery nunnery :
They blush'd, and look'd more fresh than flowers
Quicken'd of late by pearly showers,
And all because they were possess'd
But of the heat of Julia's breast :
Which, as a warm and moisten'd spring,
Gave them their ever-flourishing.

79. TO THE KING AND QUEEN UPON THEIR UNHAPPY DISTANCES.

WOE, woe to them, who, by a ball of strife,
Do, and have parted here a man and wife :
CHARLES the best husband, while MARIA strives
To be, and is, the very best of wives,
Like streams, you are divorc'd ; but 'twill come when
These eyes of mine shall see you mix again.
Thus speaks the oak here ; C. and M. shall meet,
Treading on amber, with their silver-feet,
Nor will't be long ere this accomplish'd be :
The words found true, C. M., remember me.

80. DANGERS WAIT ON KINGS.

As oft as night is banish'd by the morn,
So oft we'll think we see a king new born.

Oak, the prophetic tree.

81. THE CHEAT OF CUPID; OR, THE UNGENTLE GUEST.

ONE silent night of late,
  When every creature rested,
Came one unto my gate
  And, knocking, me molested.

Who's that, said I, beats there,
  And troubles thus the sleepy?
Cast off, said he, all fear,
  And let not locks thus keep ye.

For I a boy am, who
  By moonless nights have swerved;
And all with show'rs wet through,
  And e'en with cold half starved.

I pitiful arose,
  And soon a taper lighted;
And did myself disclose
  Unto the lad benighted.

I saw he had a bow
  And wings, too, which did shiver;
And, looking down below,
  I spied he had a quiver.

I to my chimney's shine
  Brought him, as Love professes,
And chafed his hands with mine,
  And dried his drooping tresses.

But when he felt him warm'd:
  Let's try this bow of ours,
And string, if they be harm'd,
  Said he, with these late showers.

Forthwith his bow he bent,
  And wedded string and arrow,
And struck me, that it went
  Quite through my heart and marrow.

Then, laughing loud, he flew
  Away, and thus said, flying:
Adieu, mine host, adieu,
  I'll leave thy heart a-dying.

82. TO THE REVEREND SHADE OF HIS RELIGIOUS FATHER.

That for seven lusters I did never come
To do the rites to thy religious tomb;
That neither hair was cut, or true tears shed
By me, o'er thee, as justments to the dead,
Forgive, forgive me; since I did not know
Whether thy bones had here their rest or no.
But now 'tis known, behold! behold, I bring
Unto thy ghost th' effused offering:
And look what smallage, night-shade, cypress, yew,
Unto the shades have been, or now are due,

    Seven lusters, five and thirty years.
    Hair was cut, according to the Greek custom.
    Justments, dues.
    Smallage, water parsley.

Here I devote; and something more than so;
I come to pay a debt of birth I owe.
Thou gav'st me life, but mortal; for that one
Favour I'll make full satisfaction;
For my life mortal rise from out thy hearse,
And take a life immortal from my verse.

83. DELIGHT IN DISORDER.

A SWEET disorder in the dress
Kindles in clothes a wantonness:
A lawn about the shoulders thrown
Into a fine distraction:
An erring lace which here and there
Enthralls the crimson stomacher:
A cuff neglectful, and thereby
Ribbons to flow confusedly:
A winning wave, deserving note,
In the tempestuous petticoat:
A careless shoe-string, in whose tie
I see a wild civility:
Do more bewitch me than when art
Is too precise in every part.

84. TO HIS MUSE.

WERE I to give thee baptism, I would choose
To christen thee, the bride, the bashful Muse,
Or Muse of roses: since that name does fit
Best with those virgin-verses thou hast writ:
Which are so clean, so chaste, as none may fear
Cato the censor, should he scan each here.

85. UPON LOVE.

LOVE scorch'd my finger, but did spare
    The burning of my heart;
To signify in love my share
    Should be a little part.

Little I love; but if that he
    Would but that heat recall;
That joint to ashes burnt should be,*
    Ere I would love at all.

86. TO DEAN BOURN, A RUDE RIVER IN DEVON, BY WHICH SOMETIMES HE LIVED.

DEAN BOURN, farewell; I never look to see
Dean, or thy watery † incivility.
Thy rocky bottom, that doth tear thy streams
And makes them frantic even to all extremes,
To my content I never should behold,
Were thy streams silver, or thy rocks all gold.
Rocky thou art, and rocky we discover
Thy men, and rocky are thy ways all over.
O men, O manners, now and ever known
To be a rocky generation!
A people currish, churlish as the seas,
And rude almost as rudest savages,
With whom I did, and may re-sojourn when
Rocks turn to rivers, rivers turn to men.

      * Orig. ed., *should be burnt.*
      † Orig. ed., *warty.*

87. KISSING USURY.

BIANCA, let
　　Me pay the debt
I owe thee for a kiss
　　　Thou lend'st to me,
　　And I to thee
Will render ten for this.

　　If thou wilt say
　　Ten will not pay
For that so rich a one;
　　　I'll clear the sum,
　　If it will come
Unto a million.

　　By this, I guess,
　　Of happiness
Who has a little measure,
　　　He must of right
　　To th' utmost mite
Make payment for his pleasure.

88. TO JULIA.

How rich and pleasing thou, my Julia, art
In each thy dainty and peculiar part!
First, for thy queenship, on thy head is set
Of flowers a sweet commingled coronet:
About thy neck a carcanet is bound,
Made of the ruby, pearl and diamond:

Carcanet, necklace.

A golden ring that shines upon thy thumb:
About thy wrist, the rich dardanium.*
Between thy breasts (than down of swans more white)
There plays the sapphire with the chrysolite.
No part besides must of thyself be known,
But by the topaz, opal, chalcedon.

89. TO LAURELS.

A FUNERAL stone
Or verse I covet none,
But only crave
Of you that I may have
A sacred laurel springing from my grave:
Which being seen,
Blest with perpetual green,
May grow to be
Not so much call'd a tree
As the eternal monument of me.

90. HIS CAVALIER.

GIVE me that man that dares bestride
The active sea-horse, and with pride
Through that huge field of waters ride.

Who with his looks, too, can appease
The ruffling winds and raging seas,
In midst of all their outrages.

This, this a virtuous man can do,
Sail against rocks, and split them too;
Ay, and a world of pikes pass through.

* *Dardanium,* a bracelet, from Dardanus so called.
(Note in the original edition.)

91. ZEAL REQUIRED IN LOVE.

I'LL do my best to win whene'er I woo :
That man loves not who is not zealous too.

92. THE BAG OF THE BEE.

ABOUT the sweet bag of a bee
   Two cupids fell at odds,
And whose the pretty prize should be
   They vow'd to ask the gods.

Which Venus hearing, thither came,
   And for their boldness stripp'd them,
And, taking thence from each his flame,
   With rods of myrtle whipp'd them.

Which done, to still their wanton cries,
   When quiet grown she'd seen them,
She kiss'd, and wip'd their dove-like eyes,
   And gave the bag between them.

93. LOVE KILLED BY LACK.

LET me be warm, let me be fully fed,
Luxurious love by wealth is nourished.
Let me be lean, and cold, and once grown poor,
I shall dislike what once I lov'd before.

94. TO HIS MISTRESS.

CHOOSE me your valentine,
   Next let us marry—
Love to the death will pine
   If we long tarry.

Promise, and keep your vows,
　Or vow ye never—
Love's doctrine disallows
　Troth-breakers ever.

You have broke promise twice,
　Dear, to undo me,
If you prove faithless thrice
　None then will woo ye.

95. TO THE GENEROUS READER.

SEE and not see, and if thou chance t'espy
Some aberrations in my poetry,
Wink at small faults ; the greater, ne'ertheless,
Hide, and with them their father's nakedness.
Let's do our best, our watch and ward to keep ;
Homer himself, in a long work, may sleep.

96. TO CRITICS.

I'LL write, because I'll give
You critics means to live ;
For should I not supply
The cause, th' effect would die.

97. DUTY TO TYRANTS.

GOOD princes must be pray'd for ; for the bad
They must be borne with, and in rev'rence had.
Do they first pill thee, next pluck off thy skin ?
Good children kiss the rods that punish sin.
Touch not the tyrant ; let the gods alone
To strike him dead that but usurps a throne.

　　　Pill, plunder.

98. BEING ONCE BLIND, HIS REQUEST TO BIANCA.

WHEN age or chance has made me blind,
So that the path I cannot find,
And when my falls and stumblings are
More than the stones i' th' street by far,
Go thou afore, and I shall well
Follow thy perfumes by the smell;
Or be my guide, and I shall be
Led by some light that flows from thee.
Thus held or led by thee, I shall
In ways confus'd nor slip or fall.

100. NO WANT WHERE THERE'S LITTLE.

To bread and water none is poor;
And having these, what need of more?
Though much from out the cess be spent,
Nature with little is content.

101. BARLEY-BREAK; OR, LAST IN HELL.

WE two are last in hell; what may we fear
To be tormented or kept pris'ners here?
Alas! if kissing be of plagues the worst,
We'll wish in hell we had been last and first.

Cess, the parish assessment for church purposes.

Barley-break, a country game resembling prisoners' base. See Note.

Hell, the "middle den," the occupants of which had to catch the other players.

102. THE DEFINITION OF BEAUTY.

BEAUTY no other thing is than a beam
Flashed out between the middle and extreme.

103. TO DIANEME.

DEAR, though to part it be a hell,
Yet, Dianeme, now farewell:
Thy frown last night did bid me go,
But whither only grief does know.
I do beseech thee ere we part,
If merciful as fair thou art,
Or else desir'st that maids should tell
Thy pity by love's chronicle,
O Dianeme, rather kill
Me, than to make me languish still!
'Tis cruelty in thee to th' height
Thus, thus to wound, not kill outright;
Yet there's a way found, if you please,
By sudden death to give me ease;
And thus devis'd, do thou but this—
Bequeath to me one parting kiss,
So sup'rabundant joy shall be
The executioner of me.

104. TO ANTHEA LYING IN BED.

So looks Anthea, when in bed she lies
O'ercome or half betray'd by tiffanies,
Like to a twilight, or that simpering dawn
That roses show when misted o'er with lawn.
Twilight is yet, till that her lawns give way;
Which done, that dawn turns then to perfect day.

Tiffanies, gauzes.   *Lawn*, fine linen.

105. TO ELECTRA.

MORE white than whitest lilies far,
Or snow, or whitest swans you are :
More white than are the whitest creams,
Or moonlight tinselling the streams :
More white than pearls, or Juno's thigh,
Or Pelops' arm of ivory.
True, I confess, such whites as these
May me delight, not fully please ;
Till like Ixion's cloud you be
White, warm, and soft to lie with me.

106. A COUNTRY-LIFE : TO HIS BROTHER, MR. THO. HERRICK.

THRICE, and above, bless'd, my soul's half, art thou
    In thy both last and better vow :
Could'st leave the city, for exchange, to see
    The country's sweet simplicity :
And it to know and practise, with intent
    To grow the sooner innocent
By studying to know virtue, and to aim
    More at her nature than her name.
The last is but the least ; the first doth tell
    Ways less to live than to live well :
And both are known to thee, who now can'st live
    Led by thy conscience ; to give

Pelops' arm, which Jove gave him to replace the one
eaten by Ceres at the feast of Tantalus.

Ixion's cloud, to which Jove, for his deception, gave
the form of Juno.

Justice to soon-pleased nature ; and to show
    Wisdom and she together go
And keep one centre : this with that conspires
    To teach man to confine desires
And know that riches have their proper stint
    In the contented mind, not mint :
And can'st instruct that those who have the itch
    Of craving more are never rich.
These things thou know'st to th' height, and dost
      prevent
    That plague; because thou art content
With that heav'n gave thee with a wary hand,
    More blessed in thy brass than land,
To keep cheap nature even and upright ;
    To cool, not cocker appetite.
Thus thou canst tersely live to satisfy
    The belly chiefly, not the eye ;
Keeping the barking stomach wisely quiet,
    Less with a neat than needful diet.
But that which most makes sweet thy country life
    Is the fruition of a wife :
Whom, stars consenting with thy fate, thou hast
    Got not so beautiful as chaste :
By whose warm side thou dost securely sleep,
    While love the sentinel doth keep,
With those deeds done by day, which ne'er affright
    Thy silken slumbers in the night.

        Brass, money.
        Cocker, pamper.
        Neat, dainty.

Nor has the darkness power to usher in
    Fear to those sheets that know no sin ;
But still thy wife, by chaste intentions led,
    Gives thee each night a maidenhead.
The damask'd meadows and the pebbly streams
    Sweeten and make soft your dreams :
The purling springs, groves, birds, and well-weav'd
      bowers,
    With fields enamelled with flowers,
Present their shapes ; while fantasy discloses
    Millions of lilies mix'd with roses.
Then dream ye hear the lamb by many a bleat
    Woo'd to come suck the milky teat :
While Faunus in the vision comes to keep
    From rav'ning wolves the fleecy sheep.
With thousand such enchanting dreams, that meet
    To make sleep not so sound as sweet :
Nor can these figures so thy rest endear
    As not to rise when Chanticlere
Warns the last watch ; but with the dawn dost rise
    To work, but first to sacrifice ;
Making thy peace with heav'n, for some late fault,
    With holy-meal and spirting-salt.
Which done, thy painful thumb this sentence tells
    us,
    Jove for our labour all things sells us.
Nor are thy daily and devout affairs
    Attended with those desp'rate cares

    Spirting-salt, the "saliente mica" of Horace. See
Note.

Th' industrious merchant has ; who, for to find
    Gold, runneth to the Western Inde,
And back again, tortured with fears, doth fly,
    Untaught to suffer poverty.
But thou at home, bless'd with securest ease,
    Sitt'st, and believ'st that there be seas
And watery dangers ; while thy whiter hap
    But sees these things within thy map.
And viewing them with a more safe survey
    Mak'st easy fear unto thee say,—
" *A heart thrice wall'd with oak and brass that man*
    Had, first durst plough the ocean ".
But thou at home, without or tide or gale,
    Can'st in thy map securely sail :
Seeing those painted countries, and so guess
    By those fine shades their substances :
And, from thy compass taking small advice,
    Buy'st travel at the lowest price.
Nor are thine ears so deaf but thou canst hear,
    Far more with wonder than with fear,
Fame tell of states, of countries, courts, and kings,
    And believe there be such things :
When of these truths thy happier knowledge lies
    More in thine ears than in thine eyes.
And when thou hear'st by that too true report
    Vice rules the most or all at court,
Thy pious wishes are, though thou not there,
    Virtue had, and mov'd her sphere.
But thou liv'st fearless ; and thy face ne'er shows
    Fortune when she comes or goes,
But with thy equal thoughts prepared dost stand,
    To take her by the either hand ;

Nor car'st which comes the first, the foul or fair :
  A wise man ev'ry way lies square,
And, like a surly oak with storms perplex'd,
  Grows still the stronger, strongly vex'd.
Be so, bold spirit ; stand centre-like, unmov'd ;
  And be not only thought, but prov'd
To be what I report thee ; and inure
  Thyself, if want comes to endure :
And so thou dost, for thy desires are
  Confin'd to live with private lar :
Not curious whether appetite be fed
  Or with the first or second bread,
Who keep'st no proud mouth for delicious cates :
  Hunger makes coarse meats delicates.
Canst, and unurg'd, forsake that larded fare,
  Which art, not nature, makes so rare,
To taste boil'd nettles, colworts, beets, and eat
  These and sour herbs as dainty meat,
While soft opinion makes thy Genius say,
  Content makes all ambrosia.
Nor is it that thou keep'st this stricter size
  So much for want as exercise :
To numb the sense of dearth, which should sin
    haste it,
  Thou might'st but only see't, not taste it.
Yet can thy humble roof maintain a choir
  Of singing crickets by the fire :

Lar, the "closet-gods," or gods of the house.
Colworts, cabbages.
Size or *assize*, a fixed allowance of food, a ration.

And the brisk mouse may feast herself with crumbs
   Till that the green-eyed kitling comes,
Then to her cabin blest she can escape
   The sudden danger of a rape :
And thus thy little well-kept stock doth prove
   Wealth cannot make a life, but love.
Nor art thou so close-handed but canst spend,
   Counsel concurring with the end,
As well as spare, still conning o'er this theme,
   To shun the first and last extreme.
Ordaining that thy small stock find no breach,
   Or to exceed thy tether's reach :
But to live round, and close, and wisely true
   To thine own self, and known to few.
Thus let thy rural sanctuary be
   Elysium to thy wife and thee ;
There to disport yourselves with golden measure:
   For seldom use commends the pleasure.
Live, and live blest, thrice happy pair ; let breath,
   But lost to one, be the other's death.
And as there is one love, one faith, one troth,
   Be so one death, one grave to both.
Till when, in such assurance live ye may,
   Nor fear or wish your dying day.

107. DIVINATION BY A DAFFODIL.

WHEN a daffodil I see,
Hanging down his head towards me,
Guess I may what I must be :
First, I shall decline my head ;
Secondly, I shall be dead ;
Lastly, safely buried.

108. TO THE PAINTER, TO DRAW HIM A PICTURE.

COME, skilful Lupo, now, and take
Thy bice, thy umber, pink, and lake;
And let it be thy pencil's strife,
To paint a Bridgeman to the life:
Draw him as like too, as you can,
An old, poor, lying, flattering man:
His cheeks bepimpled, red and blue;
His nose and lips of mulberry hue.
Then, for an easy fancy, place
A burling iron for his face:
Next, make his cheeks with breath to swell,
And for to speak, if possible:
But do not so, for fear lest he
Should by his breathing, poison thee.

111. A LYRIC TO MIRTH.

WHILE the milder fates consent,
Let's enjoy our merriment:
Drink, and dance, and pipe, and play;
Kiss our dollies night and day:
Crowned with clusters of the vine,
Let us sit, and quaff our wine.
Call on Bacchus, chant his praise;
Shake the thyrse, and bite the bays:

Bice, properly a brown grey, but by transference from "blue bice" and "green bice," used for blue and green.

Burling iron, pincers for extracting knots.

Rouse Anacreon from the dead,
And return him drunk to bed:
Sing o'er Horace, for ere long
Death will come and mar the song:
Then shall Wilson and Gotiere
Never sing or play more here.

112. TO THE EARL OF WESTMORELAND.

WHEN my date's done, and my grey age must die,
Nurse up, great lord, this my posterity:
Weak though it be, long may it grow and stand,
Shored up by you, brave Earl of Westmoreland.

113. AGAINST LOVE.

WHENE'ER my heart love's warmth but entertains,
Oh frost! oh snow! oh hail! forbid the banes.
One drop now deads a spark, but if the same
Once gets a force, floods cannot quench the flame.
Rather than love, let me be ever lost,
Or let me 'gender with eternal frost.

114. UPON JULIA'S RIBAND.

As shows the air when with a rainbow grac'd,
So smiles that riband 'bout my Julia's waist:
Or like—nay 'tis that zonulet of love,
Wherein all pleasures of the world are wove.

Wilson, Dr. John Wilson, the singer and composer,
one of the king's musicians (1594-1673).

Gotiere, Jacques Gaultier, a French lutist at the court
of Charles I.

115. THE FROZEN ZONE; OR, JULIA DISDAINFUL.

WHITHER? say, whither shall I fly,
To slack these flames wherein I fry?
To the treasures, shall I go,
Of the rain, frost, hail, and snow?
Shall I search the underground,
Where all damps and mists are found?
Shall I seek (for speedy ease)
All the floods and frozen seas?
Or descend into the deep,
Where eternal cold does keep?
These may cool; but there's a zone
Colder yet than anyone:
That's my Julia's breast, where dwells
Such destructive icicles,
As that the congelation will
Me sooner starve than those can kill.

116. AN EPITAPH UPON A SOBER MATRON.

WITH blameless carriage, I lived here
To the almost seven and fortieth year.
Stout sons I had, and those twice three
One only daughter lent to me:
The which was made a happy bride
But thrice three moons before she died.
My modest wedlock, that was known
Contented with the bed of one,

117. TO THE PATRON OF POETS, M. END. PORTER.

Let there be patrons, patrons like to thee,
Brave Porter! poets ne'er will wanting be:
Fabius and Cotta, Lentulus, all live
In thee, thou man of men! who here do'st give
Not only subject-matter for our wit,
But likewise oil of maintenance to it:
For which, before thy threshold, we'll lay down
Our thyrse for sceptre, and our bays for crown.
For, to say truth, all garlands are thy due:
The laurel, myrtle, oak, and ivy too.

118. THE SADNESS OF THINGS FOR SAPPHO'S SICKNESS.

Lilies will languish; violets look ill;
Sickly the primrose; pale the daffodil;
That gallant tulip will hang down his head,
Like to a virgin newly ravished;
Pansies will weep, and marigolds will wither,
And keep a fast and funeral together;
    Sappho droop, daisies will open never,
But bid good-night, and close their lids for ever.

119. LEANDER'S OBSEQUIES.

When as Leander young was drown'd
No heart by Love receiv'd a wound,
But on a rock himself sat by,
There weeping sup'rabundantly.
Sighs numberless he cast about,
And, all his tapers thus put out,
His head upon his hand he laid,
And sobbing deeply, thus he said:

4

" Ah, cruel sea," and, looking on't,
Wept as he'd drown the Hellespont.
And sure his tongue had more express'd
But that his tears forbade the rest.

120. HOPE HEARTENS.

NONE goes to warfare but with this intent—
The gains must dead the fears of detriment.

121. FOUR THINGS MAKE US HAPPY HERE.

HEALTH is the first good lent to men ;
A gentle disposition then :
Next, to be rich by no by-ways ;
Lastly, with friends t'enjoy our days.

122. HIS PARTING FROM MRS. DOROTHY KENNEDY.

WHEN I did go from thee I felt that smart
Which bodies do when souls from them depart.
Thou did'st not mind it ; though thou then might'st
    see
Me turn'd to tears ; yet did'st not weep for me.
'Tis true, I kiss'd thee ; but I could not hear
Thee spend a sigh t'accompany my tear.
Methought 'twas strange that thou so hard should'st
    prove,
Whose heart, whose hand, whose every part spake
    love.
Prithee, lest maids should censure thee, but say
Thou shed'st one tear, whenas I went away ;
And that will please me somewhat : though I know,
And Love will swear't, my dearest did not so.

123. THE TEAR SENT TO HER FROM STAINES.

GLIDE, gentle streams, and bear
Along with you my tear
  To that coy girl
  Who smiles, yet slays
  Me with delays,
And strings my tears as pearl.

See! see, she's yonder set,
Making a carcanet
  Of maiden-flowers!
  There, there present
  This orient
And pendant pearl of ours.

Then say I've sent one more
Gem to enrich her store ;
  And that is all
  Which I can send,
  Or vainly spend,
For tears no more will fall.

Nor will I seek supply
Of them, the spring's once dry;
  But I'll devise,
  Among the rest,
  A way that's best
How I may save mine eyes.

Yet say—should she condemn
Me to surrender them—

  Carcanet, necklace.

Then say my part
Must be to weep
Out them, to keep .
A poor, yet loving heart.

Say too, she would have this;
She shall: then my hope is,
That when I'm poor
And nothing have
To send or save,
I'm sure she'll ask no more.

124. UPON ONE LILY, WHO MARRIED WITH A MAID CALLED ROSE.

WHAT times of sweetness this fair day foreshows,
Whenas the Lily marries with the Rose!
What next is look'd for? but we all should see
To spring from thee a sweet posterity.

125. AN EPITAPH UPON A CHILD.

VIRGINS promis'd when I died
That they would each primrose-tide
Duly, morn and evening, come,
And with flowers dress my tomb.
Having promis'd, pay your debts,
Maids, and here strew violets.

127. THE HOUR-GLASS.

THAT hour-glass which there you see
With water fill'd, sirs, credit me,

The humour was, as I have read,
But lovers' tears incrystalled.
Which, as they drop by drop do pass
From th' upper to the under-glass,
Do in a trickling manner tell,
By many a watery syllable,
That lovers' tears in lifetime shed
Do restless run when they are dead.

128. HIS FAREWELL TO SACK.

FAREWELL thou thing, time past so known, so dear
To me as blood to life and spirit; near,
Nay, thou more near than kindred, friend, man, wife,
Male to the female, soul to body; life
To quick action, or the warm soft side
Of the resigning, yet resisting bride.
The kiss of virgins, first fruits of the bed,
Soft speech, smooth touch, the lips, the maidenhead :
These and a thousand sweets could never be
So near or dear as thou wast once to me.
O thou, the drink of gods and angels ! wine
That scatter'st spirit and lust, whose purest shine
More radiant than the summer's sunbeams shows ;
Each way illustrious, brave, and like to those
Comets we see by night, whose shagg'd portents
Foretell the coming of some dire events,

Humour, moisture.
Shagg'd, rough-haired.

Or some full flame which with a pride aspires,
Throwing about his wild and active fires ;
'Tis thou, above nectar, O divinest soul !
Eternal in thyself, that can'st control
That which subverts whole nature, grief and care,
Vexation of the mind, and damn'd despair.
'Tis thou alone who, with thy mystic fan,
Work'st more than wisdom, art, or nature can
To rouse the sacred madness and awake
The frost-bound blood and spirits, and to make
Them frantic with thy raptures flashing through
The soul like lightning, and as active too.
'Tis not Apollo can, or those thrice three
Castalian sisters, sing, if wanting thee.
Horace, Anacreon, both had lost their fame,
Had'st thou not fill'd them with thy fire and flame.
Phœbean splendour ! and thou, Thespian spring !
Of which sweet swans must drink before they sing
Their true-pac'd numbers and their holy lays,
Which makes them worthy cedar and the bays.
But why, why longer do I gaze upon
Thee with the eye of admiration ?
Since I must leave thee, and enforc'd must say
To all thy witching beauties, Go, away.
But if thy whimpering looks do ask me why,
Then know that nature bids thee go, not I.
'Tis her erroneous self has made a brain

Mystic fan, the " mystica vannus Iacchi " of Georgic, i. 166.

Cedar, *i.e.*, cedar oil, used for the preservation of manuscripts.

Uncapable of such a sovereign
As is thy powerful self.   Prithee not smile,
Or smile more inly, lest thy looks beguile
My vows denounc'd in zeal, which thus much show
 thee
That I have sworn but by thy looks to know thee.
Let others drink thee freely, and desire
Thee and their lips espous'd, while I admire
And love thee, but not taste thee.   Let my muse
Fail of thy former helps, and only use
Her inadult'rate strength : what's done by me
Hereafter shall smell of the lamp, not thee.

130. UPON MRS. ELIZABETH WHEELER, UNDER THE NAME OF AMARILLIS.

SWEET Amarillis by a spring's
Soft and soul-melting murmurings
Slept, and thus sleeping, thither flew
A robin-redbreast, who, at view,
Not seeing her at all to stir,
Brought leaves and moss to cover her ;
But while he perking there did pry
About the arch of either eye,
The lid began to let out day,
At which poor robin flew away,
And seeing her not dead, but all disleav'd,
He chirp'd for joy to see himself deceiv'd.

132. TO MYRRHA, HARD-HEARTED.

FOLD now thine arms and hang the head,
Like to a lily withered;
Next look thou like a sickly moon,
Or like Jocasta in a swoon;
Then weep and sigh and softly go,
Like to a widow drown'd in woe,
Or like a virgin full of ruth
For the lost sweetheart of her youth;
And all because, fair maid, thou art
Insensible of all my smart,
And of those evil days that be
Now posting on to punish thee.
The gods are easy, and condemn
All such as are not soft like them.

133. THE EYE.

MAKE me a heaven, and make me there
Many a less and greater sphere:
Make me the straight and oblique lines,
The motions, lations and the signs.
Make me a chariot and a sun,
And let them through a zodiac run;
Next place me zones and tropics there,
With all the seasons of the year.
Make me a sunset and a night,
And then present the morning's light
Cloth'd in her chamlets of delight.

Lations, astral attractions.
Chamlets, i.e., camlets, stuffs made from camels' hair.

To these make clouds to pour down rain,
With weather foul, then fair again.
And when, wise artist, that thou hast
With all that can be this heaven grac't,
Ah! what is then this curious sky
But only my Corinna's eye?

134. UPON THE MUCH-LAMENTED MR. J. WARR.

WHAT wisdom, learning, wit or worth
Youth or sweet nature could bring forth
Rests here with him who was the fame,
The volume of himself and name.
If, reader, then, thou wilt draw near
And do an honour to thy tear,
Weep then for him for whom laments
Not one, but many monuments.

136. THE SUSPICION UPON HIS OVER-MUCH FAMILIA-
RITY WITH A GENTLEWOMAN.

AND must we part, because some say
Loud is our love, and loose our play,
And more than well becomes the day?
Alas for pity! and for us
Most innocent, and injured thus!
Had we kept close, or played within,
Suspicion now had been the sin,
And shame had followed long ere this,
T' have plagued what now unpunished is.
But we, as fearless of the sun,

As faultless, will not wish undone
What now is done, since *where no sin*
Unbolts the door, no shame comes in.
Then, comely and most fragrant maid,
Be you more wary than afraid
Of these reports, because you see
The fairest most suspected be.
The common forms have no one eye
Or ear of burning jealousy
To follow them: but chiefly where
Love makes the cheek and chin a sphere
To dance and play in, trust me, there
Suspicion questions every hair.
Come, you are fair, and should be seen
While you are in your sprightful green:
And what though you had been embraced
By me—were you for that unchaste?
No, no ! no more than is yond' moon
Which, shining in her perfect noon,
In all that great and glorious light,
Continues cold as is the night.
Then, beauteous maid, you may retire;
And as for me, my chaste desire
Shall move towards you, although I see
Your face no more.　So live you free
From fame's black lips, as you from me.

137. SINGLE LIFE MOST SECURE.

SUSPICION, discontent, and strife
Come in for dowry with a wife.

138. THE CURSE. A SONG.

Go, perjured man ; and if thou e'er return
To see the small remainders in mine urn,
When thou shalt laugh at my religious dust,
And ask : where's now the colour, form and trust
Of woman's beauty ? and with hand more rude
Rifle the flowers which the virgins strewed :
Know I have prayed to Fury that some wind
May blow my ashes up, and strike thee blind.

139. THE WOUNDED CUPID. SONG.

Cupid, as he lay among
Roses, by a bee was stung ;
Whereupon, in anger flying
To his mother, said thus, crying :
Help ! oh help ! your boy's a-dying.
And why, my pretty lad, said she ?
Then, blubbering, replied he :
A winged snake has bitten me,
Which country people call a bee.
At which she smiled ; then, with her hairs
And kisses drying up his tears :
Alas ! said she, my wag, if this
Such a pernicious torment is,
Come tell me then, how great's the smart
Of those thou woundest with thy dart !

140. TO DEWS. A SONG.

I BURN, I burn; and beg of you
To quench or cool me with your dew.
I fry in fire, and so consume,
Although the pile be all perfume.
Alas! the heat and death's the same,
Whether by choice or common flame,
To be in oil of roses drowned,
Or water; where's the comfort found?
Both bring one death; and I die here
Unless you cool me with a tear:
Alas! I call; but ah! I see
Ye cool and comfort all but me.

141. SOME COMFORT IN CALAMITY.

To conquered men, some comfort 'tis to fall
By the hand of him who is the general.

142. THE VISION.

SITTING alone, as one forsook,
Close by a silver-shedding brook,
With hands held up to love, I wept;
And after sorrows spent I slept:
Then in a vision I did see
A glorious form appear to me:
A virgin's face she had; her dress
Was like a sprightly Spartaness.
A silver bow, with green silk strung,
Down from her comely shoulders hung:
And as she stood, the wanton air
Dangled the ringlets of her hair.

Her legs were such Diana shows
When, tucked up, she a-hunting goes;
With buskins shortened to descry
The happy dawning of her thigh:
Which when I saw, I made access
To kiss that tempting nakedness:
But she forbade me with a wand
Of myrtle she had in her hand:
And, chiding me, said: Hence, remove,
Herrick, thou art too coarse to love.

143. LOVE ME LITTLE, LOVE ME LONG.

You say, to me-wards your affection's strong;
Pray love me little, so you love me long.
Slowly goes far: the mean is best: desire,
Grown violent, does either die or tire.

144. UPON A VIRGIN KISSING A ROSE.

'Twas but a single rose,
   Till you on it did breathe;
But since, methinks, it shows
   Not so much rose as wreath.

145. UPON A WIFE THAT DIED MAD WITH JEALOUSY.

In this little vault she lies,
Here, with all her jealousies:
Quiet yet; but if ye make
Any noise they both will wake,
And such spirits raise 'twill then
Trouble death to lay again.

146. UPON THE BISHOP OF LINCOLN'S IMPRISONMENT.

NEVER was day so over-sick with showers
But that it had some intermitting hours;
Never was night so tedious but it knew
The last watch out, and saw the dawning too;
Never was dungeon so obscurely deep
Wherein or light or day did never peep;
Never did moon so ebb, or seas so wane,
But they left hope-seed to fill up again.
So you, my lord, though you have now your stay,
Your night, your prison, and your ebb, you may
Spring up afresh, when all these mists are spent,
And star-like, once more gild our firmament.
Let but that mighty Cæsar speak, and then
All bolts, all bars, all gates shall cleave; as when
That earthquake shook the house, and gave the stout
Apostles way, unshackled, to go out.
This, as I wish for, so I hope to see ;
Though you, my lord, have been unkind to me,
To wound my heart, and never to apply,
When you had power, the meanest remedy.
Well, though my grief by you was gall'd the more,
Yet I bring balm and oil to heal your sore.

147. DISSUASIONS FROM IDLENESS.

CYNTHIUS, pluck ye by the ear,
That ye may good doctrine hear ;
Play not with the maiden-hair,
For each ringlet there's a snare.

Cheek, and eye, and lip, and chin—
These are traps to take fools in.
Arms, and hands, and all parts else,
Are but toils, or manacles,
Set on purpose to enthral
Men, but slothfuls most of all.
Live employed, and so live free
From these fetters; like to me,
Who have found, and still can prove,
The lazy man the most doth love.

149. AN EPITHALAMY TO SIR THOMAS SOUTHWELL AND HIS LADY.

I.

Now, now's the time, so oft by truth
Promis'd should come to crown your youth.
 Then, fair ones, do not wrong
 Your joys by staying long;
 Or let love's fire go out,
 By lingering thus in doubt;
 But learn that time once lost
 Is ne'er redeem'd by cost.
Then away; come, Hymen, guide
To the bed the bashful bride.

II.

Is it, sweet maid, your fault these holy
Bridal rites go on so slowly?
 Dear, is it this you dread
 The loss of maidenhead?

Believe me, you will most
Esteem it when 'tis lost;
Then it no longer keep,
Lest issue lie asleep.
Then, away; come, Hymen, guide
To the bed the bashful bride.

III.

These precious, pearly, purling tears
But spring from ceremonious fears.
And 'tis but native shame
That hides the loving flame,
And may a while control
The soft and am'rous soul;
But yet love's fire will waste
Such bashfulness at last.
Then, away; come, Hymen, guide
To the bed the bashful bride.

IV.

Night now hath watch'd herself half blind,
Yet not a maidenhead resign'd!
'Tis strange, ye will not fly
To love's sweet mystery.
Might yon full moon the sweets
Have, promised to your sheets,
She soon would leave her sphere,
To be admitted there.
Then, away; come, Hymen, guide
To the bed the bashful bride.

V.

On, on devoutly, make no stay;
While Domiduca leads the way,
    And Genius, who attends
    The bed for lucky ends.
    With Juno goes the Hours
    And Graces strewing flowers.
    And the boys with sweet tunes sing:
    Hymen, O' Hymen, bring
Home the turtles; Hymen, guide
To the bed the bashful bride.

VI.

Behold! how Hymen's taper-light
Shows you how much is spent of night.
    See, see the bridegroom's torch
    Half wasted in the porch.
    And now those tapers five,
    That show the womb shall thrive,
    Their silv'ry flames advance,
    To tell all prosp'rous chance
Still shall crown the happy life
Of the goodman and the wife.

VII.

Move forward then your rosy feet,
And make whate'er they touch turn sweet.
    May all, like flowery meads,
    Smell where your soft foot treads;
    And everything assume

Domiduca, Juno, the goddess of marriage, the "home-bringer".

5

To it the like perfume,
As Zephyrus when he 'spires
Through woodbine and sweetbriars.
Then, away; come, Hymen, guide
To the bed the bashful bride.

VIII.

And now the yellow veil at last
Over her fragrant cheek is cast.
Now seems she to express
A bashful willingness:
Showing a heart consenting,
As with a will repenting.
Then gently lead her on
With wise suspicion ;
For that, matrons say, a measure
Of that passion sweetens pleasure.

IX.

You, you that be of her nearest kin,
Now o'er the threshold force her in.
But to avert the worst
Let her her fillets first
Knit to the posts, this point
Remembering, to anoint
The sides, for 'tis a charm
Strong against future harm ;
And the evil deads, the which
There was hidden by the witch.

X.

O Venus ! thou to whom is known
The best way how to loose the zone

Of virgins, tell the maid
She need not be afraid,
And bid the youth apply
Close kisses if she cry,
And charge he not forbears
Her though she woo with tears.
Tell them now they must adventure,
Since that love and night bid enter.

XI.

No fatal owl the bedstead keeps,
With direful notes to fright your sleeps;
    No furies here about
    To put the tapers out,
    Watch or did make the bed:
    'Tis omen full of dread;
    But all fair signs appear
    Within the chamber here.
Juno here far off doth stand,
Cooling sleep with charming wand.

XII.

Virgins, weep not; 'twill come when,
As she, so you'll be ripe for men.
    Then grieve her not with saying
    She must no more a-maying,
    Or by rosebuds divine
    Who'll be her valentine.
    Nor name those wanton reaks
    You've had at barley-breaks,

Reaks, pranks.   *Barley-break*, a country game, see 101.

But now kiss her and thus say,
" Take time, lady, while ye may ".

XIII.

Now bar the doors; the bridegroom puts
The eager boys to gather nuts.
    And now both love and time
    To their full height do climb:
    Oh! give them active heat
    And moisture both complete:
    Fit organs for increase,
    To keep and to release
That which may the honour'd stem
Circle with a diadem.

XIV.

And now, behold! the bed or couch
That ne'er knew bride's or bridegroom's touch,
    Feels in itself a fire;
    And, tickled with desire,
    Pants with a downy breast,
    As with a heart possesst,
    Shrugging as it did move
    Ev'n with the soul of love.
And, oh! had it but a tongue,
Doves, 'twould say, ye bill too long.

XV.

O enter then! but see ye shun
A sleep until the act be done.
    Let kisses in their close,
    Breathe as the damask rose,

Or sweet as is that gum
Doth from Panchaia come.
Teach nature now to know
Lips can make cherries grow
Sooner than she ever yet
In her wisdom could beget.

XVI.

On your minutes, hours, days, months, years,
Drop the fat blessing of the spheres.
    That good which heav'n can give
    To make you bravely live
    Fall like a spangling dew
    By day and night on you.
    May fortune's lily-hand
    Open at your command;
With all lucky birds to side
With the bridegroom and the bride.

XVII.

Let bounteous Fate[s] your spindles full
Fill, and wind up with whitest wool.
    Let them not cut the thread
    Of life until ye bid.
    May death yet come at last,
    And not with desp'rate haste,
    But when ye both can say
    " Come, let us now away,"
Be ye to the barn then borne,
Two, like two ripe shocks of corn.

Panchaia, the land of spices : *cf.* Virg. G. ii. 139; Aen.
iv. 379.

150. TEARS ARE TONGUES.

WHEN Julia chid I stood as mute the while
As is the fish or tongueless crocodile.
Air coin'd to words my Julia could not hear,
But she could see each eye to stamp a tear;
By which mine angry mistress might descry
Tears are the noble language of the eye.
And when true love of words is destitute
The eyes by tears speak, while the tongue is mute.

151. UPON A YOUNG MOTHER OF MANY CHILDREN.

LET all chaste matrons, when they chance to see
My num'rous issue, praise and pity me:
Praise me for having such a fruitful womb,
Pity me, too, who found so soon a tomb.

152. TO ELECTRA.

I'LL come to thee in all those shapes
As Jove did when he made his rapes,
Only I'll not appear to thee
As he did once to Semele.
Thunder and lightning I'll lay by,
To talk with thee familiarly.
Which done, then quickly we'll undress
To one and th' other's nakedness.
And, ravish'd, plunge into the bed,
Bodies and souls commingled,
And kissing, so as none may hear,
We'll weary all the fables there.

Fables, i.e., of Jove's amours.

153. HIS WISH.

IT is sufficient if we pray
To Jove, who gives and takes away:
Let him the land and living find;
Let me alone to fit the mind.

154. HIS PROTESTATION TO PERILLA.

NOONDAY and midnight shall at once be seen:
Trees, at one time, shall be both sere and green:
Fire and water shall together lie
In one self-sweet-conspiring sympathy:
Summer and winter shall at one time show
Ripe ears of corn, and up to th' ears in snow:
Seas shall be sandless; fields devoid of grass;
Shapeless the world, as when all chaos was,
Before, my dear Perilla, I will be
False to my vow, or fall away from thee.

155. LOVE PERFUMES ALL PARTS.

IF I kiss Anthea's breast,
There I smell the phœnix nest:
If her lip, the most sincere
Altar of incense I smell there—
Hands, and thighs, and legs are all
Richly aromatical.
Goddess Isis can't transfer
Musks and ambers more from her:
Nor can Juno sweeter be,
When she lies with Jove, than she.

156. TO JULIA.

Permit me, Julia, now to go away ;
Or by thy love decree me here to stay.
If thou wilt say that I shall live with thee,
Here shall my endless tabernacle be :
If not, as banish'd, I will live alone
There where no language ever yet was known

157. ON HIMSELF.

Love-sick I am, and must endure
A desperate grief, that finds no cure.
Ah me ! I try ; and trying, prove
No herbs have power to cure love.
Only one sovereign salve I know,
And that is death, the end of woe.

158. VIRTUE IS SENSIBLE OF SUFFERING.

Though a wise man all pressures can sustain,
His virtue still is sensible of pain :
Large shoulders though he has, and well can bear,
He feels when packs do pinch him, and the where.

159. THE CRUEL MAID.

And cruel maid, because I see
You scornful of my love and me,

I'll trouble you no more; but go
My way where you shall never know
What is become of me: there I
Will find me out a path to die,
Or learn some way how to forget
You and your name for ever: yet,
Ere I go hence, know this from me,
What will, in time, your fortune be:
This to your coyness I will tell,
And, having spoke it once, farewell.
The lily will not long endure,
Nor the snow continue pure;
The rose, the violet, one day,
See, both these lady-flowers decay:
And you must fade as well as they.
And it may chance that Love may turn,
And, like to mine, make your heart burn
And weep to see't; yet this thing do,
That my last vow commends to you:
When you shall see that I am dead,
For pity let a tear be shed;
And, with your mantle o'er me cast,
Give my cold lips a kiss at last:
If twice you kiss you need not fear
That I shall stir or live more here.
Next, hollow out a tomb to cover
Me—me, the most despisèd lover,
And write thereon: *This, reader, know:*
Love kill'd this man. No more, but so.

160. TO DIANEME.

SWEET, be not proud of those two eyes
Which, starlike, sparkle in their skies ;
Nor be you proud that you can see
All hearts your captives, yours yet free ;
Be you not proud of that rich hair
Which wantons with the love-sick air ;
Whenas that ruby which you wear,
Sunk from the tip of your soft ear,
Will last to be a precious stone
When all your world of beauty's gone.

161. TO THE KING, TO CURE THE EVIL.

To find that tree of life whose fruits did feed
And leaves did heal all sick of human seed :
To find Bethesda and an angel there
Stirring the waters, I am come ; and here,
At last, I find (after my much to do)
The tree, Bethesda and the angel too :
And all in your blest hand, which has the powers
Of all those suppling-healing herbs and flowers.
To that soft charm, that spell, that magic bough,
That high enchantment, I betake me now,
And to that hand (the branch of heaven's fair tree),
I kneel for help ; O ! lay that hand on me,
Adored Cæsar ! and my faith is such
I shall be heal'd if that my king but touch.
The evil is not yours : my sorrow sings,
" Mine is the evil, but the cure the king's ".

162. HIS MISERY IN A MISTRESS.

WATER, water I espy;
Come and cool ye, all who fry
In your loves; but none as I.

Though a thousand showers be
Still a-falling, yet I see
Not one drop to light on me.

Happy you who can have seas
For to quench ye, or some ease
From your kinder mistresses.

I have one, and she alone,
Of a thousand thousand known,
Dead to all compassion.

Such an one as will repeat
Both the cause and make the heat
More by provocation great.

Gentle friends, though I despair
Of my cure, do you beware
Of those girls which cruel are.

164. TO A GENTLEWOMAN OBJECTING TO HIM
HIS GRAY HAIRS.

AM I despised because you say,
And I dare swear, that I am gray?
Know, lady, you have but your day:
And time will come when you shall wear
Such frost and snow upon your hair;

And when (though long, it comes to pass)
You question with your looking-glass;
And in that sincere crystal seek,
But find no rose-bud in your cheek:
Nor any bed to give the show
Where such a rare carnation grew.
Ah! then too late, close in your chamber keeping,
      It will be told
      That you are old,
By those true tears y'are weeping.

165. TO CEDARS.

IF 'mongst my many poems I can see
One only worthy to be wash'd by thee,
I live for ever, let the rest all lie
In dens of darkness or condemn'd to die.

166. UPON CUPID.

LOVE like a gipsy lately came,
    And did me much importune
To see my hand, that by the same
    He might foretell my fortune.

He saw my palm, and then, said he,
    I tell thee by this score here,

Cedars, oil of cedar was used for preserving manuscripts (carmina linenda cedro. *Hor.* Ars Poet., 331.)

That thou within few months shalt be
   The youthful Prince d'Amour here.

I smil'd, and bade him once more prove,
   And by some cross-line show it,
That I could ne'er be prince of love,
   Though here the princely poet.

167. HOW PRIMROSES CAME GREEN.

VIRGINS, time-past, known were these,
Troubled with green-sicknesses :
Turn'd to flowers, still the hue,
Sickly girls, they bear of you.

168. TO JOS., LORD BISHOP OF EXETER.

WHOM should I fear to write to if I can
Stand before you, my learn'd diocesan ?
And never show blood-guiltiness or fear
To see my lines excathedrated here.
Since none so good are but you may condemn,
Or here so bad but you may pardon them.
If then, my lord, to sanctify my muse
One only poem out of all you'll choose,
And mark it for a rapture nobly writ,
'Tis good confirm'd, for you have bishop'd it.

Bloodguiltiness, guilt betrayed by blushing ; cp. **837.**
Excathedrated, condemned *ex cathedra.*

169. UPON A BLACK TWIST ROUNDING THE ARM OF
THE COUNTESS OF CARLISLE.

I SAW about her spotless wrist,
Of blackest silk, a curious twist;
Which, circumvolving gently, there
Enthrall'd her arm as prisoner.
Dark was the jail, but as if light
Had met t'engender with the night;
Or so as darkness made a stay
To show at once both night and day.
One fancy more! but if there be
Such freedom in captivity,
I beg of Love that ever I
May in like chains of darkness lie.

170. ON HIMSELF.

I FEAR no earthly powers,
But care for crowns of flowers;
And love to have my beard
With wine and oil besmear'd.
This day I'll drown all sorrow:
Who knows to live to-morrow?

172. A RING PRESENTED TO JULIA.

JULIA, I bring
To thee this ring,
Made for thy finger fit;
To show by this
That our love is
(Or should be) like to it.

Close though it be
The joint is free ;
So, when love's yoke is on,
It must not gall,
Or fret at all
With hard oppression.

But it must play
Still either way,
And be, too, such a yoke
As not too wide
To overslide,
Or be so strait to choke.

So we who bear
This beam must rear
Ourselves to such a height
As that the stay
Of either may
Create the burden light.

And as this round
Is nowhere found
To flaw, or else to sever :
So let our love
As endless prove,
And pure as gold for ever.

173. TO THE DETRACTOR.

WHERE others love and praise my verses, still
Thy long black thumb-nail marks them out for ill:
A fellon take it, or some whitflaw come
For to unslate or to untile that thumb!
But cry thee mercy: exercise thy nails
To scratch or claw, so that thy tongue not rails:
Some numbers prurient are, and some of these
Are wanton with their itch; scratch, and 'twill please.

174. UPON THE SAME.

I ASK'D thee oft what poets thou hast read,
And lik'st the best.   Still thou reply'st: The dead.
I shall, ere long, with green turfs cover'd be;
Then sure thou'lt like or thou wilt envy me.

175. JULIA'S PETTICOAT.

THY azure robe I did behold
As airy as the leaves of gold,
Which, erring here, and wandering there,
Pleas'd with transgression ev'rywhere:
Sometimes 'twould pant, and sigh, and heave,
As if to stir it scarce had leave:
But, having got it, thereupon
'Twould make a brave expansion.
And pounc'd with stars it showed to me

> *Fellon*, a sore, especially in the finger.
> *Whitflaw*, or whitlow.
> *Pounc'd*, sprinkled.

Like a celestial canopy.
Sometimes 'twould blaze, and then abate,
Like to a flame grown moderate:
Sometimes away 'twould wildly fling,
Then to thy thighs so closely cling
That some conceit did melt me down
As lovers fall into a swoon:
And, all confus'd, I there did lie
Drown'd in delights, but could not die.
That leading cloud I follow'd still,
Hoping t' have seen of it my fill;
But ah! I could not: should it move
To life eternal, I could love.

176. TO MUSIC.

BEGIN to charm, and, as thou strok'st mine ears
With thy enchantment, melt me into tears.
Then let thy active hand scud o'er thy lyre,
And make my spirits frantic with the fire.
That done, sink down into a silvery strain,
And make me smooth as balm and oil again.

177. DISTRUST.

To safeguard man from wrongs, there nothing must
Be truer to him than a wise distrust.
And to thyself be best this sentence known:
Hear all men speak, but credit few or none.

6

178. CORINNA'S GOING A-MAYING.

GET up, get up for shame, the blooming morn
Upon her wings presents the god unshorn.
 See how Aurora throws her fair
 Fresh-quilted colours through the air:
 Get up, sweet slug-a-bed, and see
 The dew bespangling herb and tree.
Each flower has wept and bow'd toward the east
Above an hour since: yet you not dress'd;
 Nay! not so much as out of bed?
 When all the birds have matins said
 And sung their thankful hymns, 'tis sin,
 Nay, profanation to keep in,
Whereas a thousand virgins on this day
Spring, sooner than the lark, to fetch in May.

Rise and put on your foliage, and be seen
To come forth, like the spring-time, fresh and green,
 And sweet as Flora.   Take no care
 For jewels for your gown or hair:
 Fear not; the leaves will strew
 Gems in abundance upon you:
Besides, the childhood of the day has kept,
Against you come, some orient pearls unwept;
 Come and receive them while the light
 Hangs on the dew-locks of the night:
 And Titan on the eastern hill
 Retires himself, or else stands still
Till you come forth.   Wash, dress, be brief in praying:
Few beads are best when once we go a-Maying.

   Beads, prayers.

Come, my Corinna, come ; and, coming, mark
How each field turns a street, each street a park
    Made green and trimm'd with trees : see how
    Devotion gives each house a bough
    Or branch : each porch, each door ere this
    An ark, a tabernacle is,
Made up of white-thorn neatly interwove ;
As if here were those cooler shades of love.
    Can such delights be in the street
    And open fields and we not see't ?
    Come, we'll abroad ; and let's obey
    The proclamation made for May :
And sin no more, as we have done, by staying ;
But, my Corinna, come, let's go a-Maying.

There's not a budding boy or girl this day
But is got up, and gone to bring in May.
    A deal of youth, ere this, is come
    Back, and with white-thorn laden home.
    Some have despatch'd their cakes and cream
    Before that we have left to dream :
And some have wept, and woo'd, and plighted troth,
And chose their pries , cre we can cast off sloth :
    Many a green-gown has been given ;
    Many a kiss, both odd and even :
    Many a glance too has been sent
    From out the eye, love's firmament ;
Many a jest told of the keys betraying
This night, and locks pick'd, yet we're not a-Maying.

     Left to dream, ceased dreaming.
     Green-gown, tumble on the grass.

Come, let us go while we are in our prime;
And take the harmless folly of the time.
　　We shall grow old apace, and die
　　Before we know our liberty.
　　Our life is short, and our days run
　　As fast away as does the sun;
And, as a vapour or a drop of rain,
Once lost, can ne'er be found again,
　　So when or you or I are made
　　A fable, song, or fleeting shade,
　　All love, all liking, all delight
　　Lies drowned with us in endless night.
Then while time serves, and we are but decaying,
Come, my Corinna, come, let's go a-Maying.

179. ON JULIA'S BREATH.

BREATHE, Julia, breathe, and I'll protest,
　　Nay more, I'll deeply swear,
That all the spices of the east
　　Are circumfused there.

180. UPON A CHILD. AN EPITAPH.

BUT born, and like a short delight,
I glided by my parents' sight.
That done, the harder fates denied
My longer stay, and so I died.
If, pitying my sad parents' tears,
You'll spill a tear or two with theirs,
And with some flowers my grave bestrew,
Love and they'll thank you for't.　Adieu.

　　　Circumfused, spread around.

181. A DIALOGUE BETWIXT HORACE AND LYDIA, TRANSLATED ANNO 1627, AND SET BY MR. RO. RAMSEY.

Hor. WHILE, Lydia, I was loved of thee,
    Nor any was preferred 'fore me
    To hug thy whitest neck, than I
    The Persian king lived not more happily.

Lyd. While thou no other didst affect,
    Nor Chloe was of more respect
    Than Lydia, far-famed Lydia,
    I flourished more than Roman Ilia.

Hor. Now Thracian Chloe governs me,
    Skilful i' th' harp and melody;
    For whose affection, Lydia, I
    (So fate spares her) am well content to die.

Lyd. My heart now set on fire is
    By Ornithes' son, young Calais,
    For whose commutual flames here I,
    To save his life, twice am content to die.

Hor. Say our first loves we should revoke,
    And, severed, join in brazen yoke;
    Admit I Chloe put away,
    And love again love-cast-off Lydia?

Lyd. Though mine be brighter than the star,
    Thou lighter than the cork by far,
    Rough as the Adriatic sea, yet I
    Will live with thee, or else for thee will die.

182. THE CAPTIV'D BEE, OR THE LITTLE FILCHER.

As Julia once a-slumbering lay
It chanced a bee did fly that way,
After a dew or dew-like shower,
To tipple freely in a flower.
For some rich flower he took the lip
Of Julia, and began to sip;
But when he felt he sucked from thence
Honey, and in the quintessence,
He drank so much he scarce could stir,
So Julia took the pilferer.
And thus surprised, as filchers use,
He thus began himself t' excuse:
Sweet lady-flower, I never brought
Hither the least one thieving thought;
But, taking those rare lips of yours
For some fresh, fragrant, luscious flowers,
I thought I might there take a taste,
Where so much syrup ran at waste.
Besides, know this: I never sting
The flower that gives me nourishing;
But with a kiss, or thanks, do pay
For honey that I bear away.
This said, he laid his little scrip
Of honey 'fore her ladyship:
And told her, as some tears did fall,
That that he took, and that was all.
At which she smiled, and bade him go
And take his bag; but thus much know:
When next he came a-pilfering so,
He should from her full lips derive
Honey enough to fill his hive.

185. AN ODE TO MASTER ENDYMION PORTER, UPON HIS BROTHER'S DEATH.

Not all thy flushing suns are set,
  Herrick, as yet;
Nor doth this far-drawn hemisphere
Frown and look sullen ev'rywhere.
Days may conclude in nights, and suns may rest
  As dead within the west;
Yet, the next morn, regild the fragrant east.

Alas! for me, that I have lost
  E'en all almost;
Sunk is my sight, set is my sun,
And all the loom of life undone:
The staff, the elm, the prop, the shelt'ring wall
  Whereon my vine did crawl,
Now, now blown down; needs must the old stock fall.

Yet, Porter, while thou keep'st alive,
  In death I thrive:
And like a phœnix re-aspire
From out my nard and fun'ral fire;
And as I prune my feathered youth, so I
  Do mar'l how I could die
When I had thee, my chief preserver, by.

I'm up, I'm up, and bless that hand
  Which makes me stand
Now as I do, and but for thee
I must confess I could not be.
The debt is paid; for he who doth resign
  Thanks to the gen'rous vine
Invites fresh grapes to fill his press with wine.

   Mar'l, marvel.

186. TO HIS DYING BROTHER, MASTER WILLIAM HERRICK.

LIFE of my life, 'take not so soon thy flight,
But stay the time till we have bade good-night.
Thou hast both wind and tide with thee; thy way
As soon despatch'd is by the night as day.
Let us not then so rudely henceforth go
Till we have wept, kissed, sigh'd, shook hands, or so.
There's pain in parting, and a kind of hell,
When once true lovers take their last farewell.
What! shall we two our endless leaves take here
Without a sad look or a solemn tear?
He knows not love that hath not this truth proved,
Love is most loth to leave the thing beloved.
Pay we our vows and go; yet when we part,
Then, even then, I will bequeath my heart
Into thy loving hands; for I'll keep none
To warm my breast when thou, my pulse, art gone.
No, here I'll last, and walk (a harmless shade)
About this urn wherein thy dust is laid,
To guard it so as nothing here shall be
Heavy to hurt those sacred seeds of thee.

187. THE OLIVE BRANCH.

SADLY I walk'd within the field,
To see what comfort it would yield;
And as I went my private way
An olive branch before me lay,
And seeing it I made a stay,

And took it up and view'd it ; then
Kissing the omen, said Amen ;
Be, be it so, and let this be
A divination unto me ;
That in short time my woes shall cease
And Love shall crown my end with peace.

189. TO CHERRY-BLOSSOMS.

YE may simper, blush and smile,
And perfume the air awhile ;
But, sweet things, ye must be gone,
Fruit, ye know, is coming on ;
Then, ah ! then, where is your grace,
Whenas cherries come in place ?

190. HOW LILIES CAME WHITE.

WHITE though ye be, yet, lilies, know,
From the first ye were not so ;
    But I'll tell ye
    What befell ye :
Cupid and his mother lay
In a cloud, while both did play,
He with his pretty finger press'd
The ruby niplet of her breast ;
Out of which the cream of light,
    Like to a dew,
    Fell down on you
And made ye white.

191. TO PANSIES.

Ah, cruel love! must I endure
Thy many scorns and find no cure?
Say, are thy medicines made to be
Helps to all others but to me?
I'll leave thee and to pansies come,
Comforts you'll afford me some;
You can ease my heart and do
What love could ne'er be brought unto.

192. ON GILLY-FLOWERS BEGOTTEN.

What was't that fell but now
    From that warm kiss of ours?
Look, look! by love I vow
    They were two gilly-flowers.

Let's kiss and kiss again,
    For if so be our closes
Make gilly-flowers, then
    I'm sure they'll fashion roses.

193. THE LILY IN A CRYSTAL.

You have beheld a smiling rose
    When virgins' hands have drawn
    O'er it a cobweb-lawn;
And here you see this lily shows,
    Tomb'd in a crystal stone,
More fair in this transparent case
    Than when it grew alone
    And had but single grace.

You see how cream but naked is
    Nor dances in the eye
    Without a strawberry,
Or some fine tincture like to this,
    Which draws the sight thereto
More by that wantoning with it
    Than when the paler hue
    No mixture did admit.

You see how amber through the streams
    More gently strokes the sight
    With some conceal'd delight
Than when he darts his radiant beams
    Into the boundless air;
Where either too much light his worth
    Doth all at once impair,
    Or set it little forth.

Put purple grapes or cherries in-
    To glass, and they will send
    More beauty to commend
Them from that clean and subtle skin
    Than if they naked stood,
And had no other pride at all
    But their own flesh and blood
    And tinctures natural.

Thus lily, rose, grape, cherry, cream,
    And strawberry do stir
    More love when they transfer
A weak, a soft, a broken beam,
        Tincture, colour, dye.

Than if they should discover
At full their proper excellence;
    Without some scene cast over
    To juggle with the sense.

Thus let this crystal'd lily be
    A rule how far to teach
    Your nakedness must reach;
And that no further than we see
    Those glaring colours laid
By art's wise hand, but to this end
    They should obey a shade,
    Lest they too far extend.

So though you're white as swan or snow,
    And have the power to move
    A world of men to love,
Yet when your lawns and silks shall flow,
    And that white cloud divide
Into a doubtful twilight, then,
    Then will your hidden pride
    Raise greater fires in men.

194. TO HIS BOOK.

LIKE to a bride, come forth, my book, at last,
With all thy richest jewels overcast;
Say, if there be, 'mongst many gems here, one
Deserveless of the name of paragon;
Blush not at all for that, since we have set
Some pearls on queens that have been counterfeit.

Scene, a covering.

195. UPON SOME WOMEN.

THOU who wilt not love, do this,
Learn of me what woman is.
Something made of thread and thrum,
A mere botch of all and some.
Pieces, patches, ropes of hair ;
Inlaid garbage everywhere.
Outside silk and outside lawn ;
Scenes to cheat us neatly drawn.
False in legs, and false in thighs ;
False in breast, teeth, hair, and eyes ;
False in head, and false enough ;
Only true in shreds and stuff.

196. SUPREME FORTUNE FALLS SOONEST.

WHILE leanest beasts in pastures feed,
The fattest ox the first must bleed.

197. THE WELCOME TO SACK.

So soft streams meet, so springs with gladder smiles
Meet after long divorcement by the isles ;
When love, the child of likeness, urgeth on
Their crystal natures to a union :
So meet stolen kisses, when the moony nights
Call forth fierce lovers to their wish'd delights ;

> *Thrum*, a small thread.
> *All and some*, anything and everything.

So kings and queens meet, when desire convinces
All thoughts but such as aim at getting princes,
As I meet thee.   Soul of my life and fame!
Eternal lamp of love! whose radiant flame
Out-glares the heaven's Osiris,* and thy gleams
Out-shine the splendour of his mid-day beams.
Welcome, O welcome, my illustrious spouse;
Welcome as are the ends unto my vows;
Aye! far more welcome than the happy soil
The sea-scourged merchant, after all his toil,
Salutes with tears of joy, when fires betray
The smoky chimneys of his Ithaca.
Where hast thou been so long from my embraces,
Poor pitied exile?   Tell me, did thy graces
Fly discontented hence, and for a time
Did rather choose to bless another clime?
Or went'st thou to this end, the more to move me,
By thy short absence, to desire and love thee?
Why frowns my sweet?   Why won't my saint confer
Favours on me, her fierce idolater?
Why are those looks, those looks the which have
    been
Time-past so fragrant, sickly now drawn in
Like a dull twilight?   Tell me, and the fault
I'll expiate with sulphur, hair and salt;
And, with the crystal humour of the spring,
Purge hence the guilt and kill this quarrelling.

Convinces, overcomes.
  * The sun.   (Note in the original edition.)
    Ithaca, the home of the wanderer Ulysses.

Wo't thou not smile or tell me what's amiss?
Have I been cold to hug thee, too remiss,
Too temp'rate in embracing? Tell me, has desire
To thee-ward died i' th' embers, and no fire
Left in this rak'd-up ash-heap as a mark
To testify the glowing of a spark?
Have I divorc'd thee only to combine
In hot adult'ry with another wine?
True, I confess I left thee, and appeal
'Twas done by me more to confirm my zeal
And double my affection on thee, as do those
Whose love grows more inflam'd by being foes.
But to forsake thee ever, could there be
A thought of such-like possibility?
When thou thyself dar'st say thy isles shall lack
Grapes before Herrick leaves canary sack.
Thou mak'st me airy, active to be borne,
Like Iphiclus, upon the tops of corn.
Thou mak'st me nimble, as the winged hours,
To dance and caper on the heads of flowers,
And ride the sunbeams. Can there be a thing
Under the heavenly Isis * that can bring
More love unto my life, or can present
My genius with a fuller blandishment?
Illustrious idol! could th' Egyptians seek
Help from the garlic, onion and the leek
And pay no vows to thee, who wast their best
God, and far more transcendent than the rest?

Iphiclus won the foot-race at the funeral games of
Pelias.

* The moon. (Note in the original edition.)

Had Cassius, that weak water-drinker, known
Thee in thy vine, or had but tasted one
Small chalice of thy frantic liquor, he,
As the wise Cato, had approv'd of thee.
Had not Jove's son, * that brave Tirynthian swain,
Invited to the Thesbian banquet, ta'en
Full goblets of thy gen'rous blood, his sprite
Ne'er had kept heat for fifty maids that night.
Come, come and kiss me ; love and lust commends
Thee and thy beauties; kiss, we will be friends
Too strong for fate to break us.   Look upon
Me with that full pride of complexion
As queens meet queens, or come thou unto me
As Cleopatra came to Anthony,
When her high carriage did at once present
To the triumvir love and wonderment.
Swell up my nerves with spirit; let my blood
Run through my veins like to a hasty flood.
Fill each part full of fire, active to do
What thy commanding soul shall put it to ;
And till I turn apostate to thy love,
Which here I vow to serve, do not remove
Thy fires from me, but Apollo's curse
Blast these-like actions, or a thing that's worse.
When these circumstants shall but live to see
The time that I prevaricate from thee.
Call me the son of beer, and then confine
Me to the tap, the toast, the turf; let wine

* Hercules.   (Note in the original edition.)
Circumstants, surroundings.

Ne'er shine upon me; may my numbers all
Run to a sudden death and funeral.
And last, when thee, dear spouse, I disavow,
Ne'er may prophetic Daphne crown my brow.

198. IMPOSSIBILITIES TO HIS FRIEND.

My faithful friend, if you can see
The fruit to grow up, or the tree;
If you can see the colour come
Into the blushing pear or plum;
If you can see the water grow
To cakes of ice or flakes of snow;
If you can see that drop of rain
Lost in the wild sea once again;
If you can see how dreams do creep
Into the brain by easy sleep:
Then there is hope that you may see
Her love me once who now hates me.

201. TO LIVE MERRILY AND TO TRUST TO GOOD VERSES.

Now is the time for mirth,
    Nor cheek or tongue be dumb;
For, with the flowery earth,
    The golden pomp is come.

The golden pomp is come;
    For now each tree does wear,
Made of her pap and gum,
    Rich beads of amber here.

Now reigns the rose, and now
   Th' Arabian dew besmears
My uncontrolled brow
   And my retorted hairs.

Homer, this health to thee,
   In sack of such a kind
That it would make thee see
   Though thou wert ne'er so blind.

Next, Virgil I'll call forth
   To pledge this second health
In wine, whose each cup's worth
   An Indian commonwealth.

A goblet next I'll drink
   To Ovid, and suppose,
Made he the pledge, he'd think
   The world had all one nose.

Then this immensive cup
   Of aromatic wine,
Catullus, I quaff up
   To that terse muse of thine.

Wild I am now with heat:
   O Bacchus, cool thy rays!
Or, frantic, I shall eat
   Thy thyrse and bite the bays.

Retorted, bound back, "retorto crine," *Martial.*
Immensive, measureless.

Round, round the roof does run,
   And, being ravish'd thus,
Come, I will drink a tun
   To my Propertius.

Now, to Tibullus, next,
   This flood I drink to thee :
But stay, I see a text
   That this presents to me.

Behold, Tibullus lies
   Here burnt, whose small return
Of ashes scarce suffice
   To fill a little urn.

Trust to good verses then ;
   They only will aspire
When pyramids, as men,
   Are lost i' th' funeral fire.

And when all bodies meet
   In Lethe to be drown'd,
Then only numbers sweet
   With endless life are crown'd.

202. FAIR DAYS: OR, DAWNS DECEITFUL.

FAIR was the dawn, and but e'en now the skies
Show'd like to cream inspir'd with strawberries,
But on a sudden all was chang'd and gone
That smil'd in that first sweet complexion.
Then thunder-claps and lightning did conspire
To tear the world, or set it all on fire.
What trust to things below, whenas we see,
As men, the heavens have their hypocrisy ?

203. LIPS TONGUELESS.

For my part, I never care
For those lips that tongue-tied are:
Tell-tales I would have them be
Of my mistress and of me.
Let them prattle how that I
Sometimes freeze and sometimes fry:
Let them tell how she doth move
Fore or backward in her love:
Let them speak by gentle tones,
One and th' other's passions:
How we watch, and seldom sleep;
How by willows we do weep;
How by stealth we meet, and then
Kiss, and sigh, so part again.
This the lips we will permit
For to tell, not publish it.

204. TO THE FEVER, NOT TO TROUBLE JULIA.

Thou'st dar'd too far; but, fury, now forbear
To give the least disturbance to her hair:
But less presume to lay a plait upon
Her skin's most smooth and clear expansion.
'Tis like a lawny firmament as yet,
Quite dispossess'd of either fray or fret.
Come thou not near that film so finely spread,
Where no one piece is yet unlevelled.
This if thou dost, woe to thee, fury, woe,
I'll send such frost, such hail, such sleet, and snow,

Such flesh-quakes, palsies, and such fears as shall
Dead thee to th' most, if not destroy thee all.
And thou a thousand thousand times shalt be
More shak'd thyself than she is scorch'd by thee.

205. TO VIOLETS.

WELCOME, maids-of-honour !
  You do bring
  In the spring,
And wait upon her.

She has virgins many,
  Fresh and fair ;
  Yet you are
More sweet than any.

You're the maiden posies,
  And so grac'd
  To be plac'd
'Fore damask roses.

Yet, though thus respected,
  By-and-by
  Ye do lie,
Poor girls, neglected.

207. TO CARNATIONS.   A SONG.

STAY while ye will, or go
  And leave no scent behind ye:
Yet, trust me, I shall know
  The place where I may find ye.

Within my Lucia's cheek,
  Whose livery ye wear,
Play ye at hide or seek,
  I'm sure to find ye there.

208.   TO THE VIRGINS, TO MAKE MUCH OF TIME.

GATHER ye rosebuds while ye may,
  Old time is still a-flying:
And this same flower that smiles to-day
  To-morrow will be dying.

The glorious lamp of heaven, the sun,
  The higher he's a-getting,
The sooner will his race be run,
  And nearer he's to setting.

That age is best which is the first,
  When youth and blood are warmer;
But being spent, the worse, and worst
  Times still succeed the former.

Then be not coy, but use your time,
  And while ye may go marry:
For having lost but once your prime
  You may for ever tarry.

209. SAFETY TO LOOK TO ONESELF.

For my neighbour I'll not know,
Whether high he builds or no :
Only this I'll look upon,
Firm be my foundation.
Sound or unsound, let it be !
'Tis the lot ordain'd for me.
He who to the ground does fall
Has not whence to sink at all.

210. TO HIS FRIEND, ON THE UNTUNABLE TIMES.

Play I could once ; but, gentle friend, you see
My harp hung up here on the willow tree.
Sing I could once ; and bravely, too, inspire
With luscious numbers my melodious lyre.
Draw I could once, although not stocks or stones,
Amphion-like, men made of flesh and bones,
Whither I would ; but ah ! I know not how,
I feel in me this transmutation now.
Grief, my dear friend, has first my harp unstrung,
Wither'd my hand, and palsy-struck my tongue.

211. HIS POETRY HIS PILLAR.

Only a little more
    I have to write,
    Then I'll give o'er,
And bid the world good-night.

'Tis but a flying minute
　　That I must stay,
　　Or linger in it;
And then I must away.

O time that cut'st down all
　　And scarce leav'st here
　　Memorial
Of any men that were.

How many lie forgot
　　In vaults beneath?
　　And piecemeal rot
Without a fame in death?

Behold this living stone
　　I rear for me,
　　Ne'er to be thrown
Down, envious Time, by thee.

Pillars let some set up
　　If so they please:
　　Here is my hope
And my Pyramides.

212. SAFETY ON THE SHORE.

WHAT though the sea be calm? Trust to the shore,
Ships have been drown'd where late they danc'd
　　before.

213. A PASTORAL UPON THE BIRTH OF PRINCE CHARLES. PRESENTED TO THE KING, AND SET BY MR. NIC. LANIERE.

The Speakers, Mirtillo, Amintas *and* Amarillis.

Amin. Good-day, Mirtillo. *Mirt.* And to you no
    less,
And all fair signs lead on our shepherdess.
    Amar. With all white luck to you. *Mirt.* But say,
    what news
Stirs in our sheep-walk? *Amin.* None, save that
    my ewes,
My wethers, lambs, and wanton kids are well,
Smooth, fair and fat! none better I can tell:
Or that this day Menalcas keeps a feast
For his sheep-shearers. *Mirt.* True, these are the
    least;
But, dear Amintas and sweet Amarillis,
Rest but a while here, by this bank of lilies,
And lend a gentle ear to one report
The country has. *Amin.* From whence? *Amar.*
    From whence? *Mirt.* The Court.
Three days before the shutting in of May
(With whitest wool be ever crown'd that day!)
To all our joy a sweet-fac'd child was born,
More tender than the childhood of the morn.
  Chor. Pan pipe to him, and bleats of lambs and
    sheep
Let lullaby the pretty prince asleep!

White, favourable.

Mirt. And that his birth should be more singular
At noon of day was seen a silver star,
Bright as the wise men's torch which guided them
To God's sweet babe, when born at Bethlehem;
While golden angels (some have told to me)
Sung out his birth with heavenly minstrelsy.

Amin. O rare! But is't a trespass if we three
Should wend along his babyship to see?

Mirt. Not so, not so.

Chor. But if it chance to prove
At most a fault, 'tis but a fault of love.

Amar. But, dear Mirtillo, I have heard it told
Those learned men brought incense, myrrh and gold
From countries far, with store of spices sweet,
And laid them down for offerings at his feet.

Mirt. 'Tis true, indeed: and each of us will bring
Unto our smiling and our blooming king
A neat, though not so great an offering.

Amar. A garland for my gift shall be
Of flowers ne'er suck'd by th' thieving bee;
And all most sweet; yet all less sweet than he.

Amint. And I will bear, along with you,
Leaves dropping down the honeyed dew,
With oaten pipes as sweet as new.

Mirt. And I a sheep-hook will bestow,
To have his little kingship know,
As he is prince, he's shepherd too.

Chor. Come, let's away, and quickly let's be dress'd,
And quickly give—*the swiftest grace is best.*
And when before him we have laid our treasures,
We'll bless the babe, then back to country pleasures.

214. TO THE LARK.

Good speed, for I this da͵
Betimes my matins say :
    Because I do
    Begin to woo,
    Sweet-singing lark,
    Be thou the clerk,
    And know thy when
    To say, Amen.
    And if I prove
    Bless'd in my love,
    Then thou shalt be
    High-priest to me,
    At my return,
    To incense burn ;
And so to solemnise
Love's and my sacrifice.

215. THE BUBBLE. A SONG.

To my revenge and to her desperate fears
Fly, thou made bubble of my sighs and tears.
In the wild air when thou hast rolled about,
And, like a blasting planet, found her out,
Stoop, mount, pass by to take her eye, then glare
Like to a dreadful comet in the air :
Next, when thou dost perceive her fixed sight
For thy revenge to be most opposite,
Then, like a globe or ball of wild-fire, fly,
And break thyself in shivers on her eye.

216. A MEDITATION FOR HIS MISTRESS.

You are a tulip seen to-day,
But, dearest, of so short a stay
That where you grew scarce man can say.

You are a lovely July-flower,
Yet one rude wind or ruffling shower
Will force you hence, and in an hour.

You are a sparkling rose i' th' bud,
Yet lost ere that chaste flesh and blood
Can show where you or grew or stood.

You are a full-spread, fair-set vine,
And can with tendrils love entwine,
Yet dried ere you distil your wine.

You are like balm enclosed well
In amber, or some crystal shell,
Yet lost ere you transfuse your smell.

You are a dainty violet,
Yet wither'd ere you can be set
Within the virgin's coronet.

You are the queen all flowers among,
But die you must, fair maid, ere long,
As he, the maker of this song.

217. THE BLEEDING HAND; OR, THE SPRIG OF EGLANTINE GIVEN TO A MAID.

From this bleeding hand of mine
Take this sprig of eglantine,

Which, though sweet unto your smell,
Yet the fretful briar will tell,
He who plucks the sweets shall prove
Many thorns to be in love.

218. LYRIC FOR LEGACIES.

GOLD I've none, for use or show,
Neither silver to bestow
At my death ; but this much know,
That each lyric here shall be
Of my love a legacy,
Left to all posterity.
Gentle friends, then do but please
To accept such coins as these
As my last remembrances.

219. A DIRGE UPON THE DEATH OF THE RIGHT VALIANT LORD, BERNARD STUART.

HENCE, hence, profane ! soft silence let us have
While we this trental sing about thy grave.

Had wolves or tigers seen but thee,
They would have showed civility ;
And, in compassion of thy years,
Washed those thy purple wounds with tears.
But since thou'rt slain, and in thy fall
The drooping kingdom suffers all ;

Trental, a dirge ; but see Note.

Chor. This we will do, we'll daily come
   And offer tears upon thy tomb:
   And if that they will not suffice,
   Thou shalt have souls for sacrifice.
Sleep in thy peace, while we with spice perfume thee,
And cedar wash thee, that no times consume thee.

  Live, live thou dost, and shalt; for why?
  Souls do not with their bodies die:
  Ignoble offsprings, they may fall
  Into the flames of funeral:
  Whenas the chosen seed shall spring
  Fresh, and for ever flourishing.

Chor. And times to come shall, weeping, read thy
   glory
   Less in these marble stones than in thy
   story.

220. TO PERENNA, A MISTRESS.

DEAR Perenna, prithee come
And with smallage dress my tomb:
Add a cypress sprig thereto,
With a tear, and so Adieu.

Cedar, oil of cedar.
Smallage, water-parsley.

223. THE FAIRY TEMPLE; OR, OBERON'S CHAPEL
·DEDICATED TO MR. JOHN MERRIFIELD, COUN-
SELLOR-AT-LAW.

RARE temples thou hast seen, I know,
And rich for in and outward show:
Survey this chapel, built alone,
Without or lime, or wood, or stone:
Then say if one thou'st seen more fine
Than this, the fairies' once, now thine.

THE TEMPLE.

A WAY enchased with glass and beads
There is, that to the chapel leads:
Whose structure, for his holy rest,
Is here the halcyon's curious nest:
Into the which who looks shall see
His temple of idolatry,
Where he of godheads has such store,
As Rome's pantheon had not more.
His house of Rimmon this he calls,
Girt with small bones instead of walls.
First, in a niche, more black than jet,
His idol-cricket there is set:
Then in a polished oval by
There stands his idol-beetle-fly:
Next in an arch, akin to this,
His idol-canker seated is:

Halcyon, king-fisher.

Then in a round is placed by these
His golden god, Cantharides.
So that, where'er ye look, ye see,
No capital, no cornice free,
Or frieze, from this fine frippery.
Now this the fairies would have known,
Theirs is a mixed religion :
And some have heard the elves it call
Part pagan, part papistical.
If unto me all tongues were granted,
I could not speak the saints here painted.
Saint Tit, Saint Nit, Saint Is, Saint Itis,
Who 'gainst Mab's-state placed here right is ;
Saint Will o' th' Wisp, of no great bigness,
But *alias* called here *Fatuus ignis;*
Saint Frip, Saint Trip, Saint Fill, Saint Fillie
Neither those other saintships will I
Here go about for to recite
Their number, almost infinite,
Which one by one here set down are
In this most curious calendar.
First, at the entrance of the gate
A little puppet-priest doth wait,
Who squeaks to all the comers there :
"*Favour your tongues who enter here ;*
Pure hands bring hither without stain."
A second pules : "*Hence, hence, profane!*"
Hard by, i' th' shell of half a nut,

> *Saint Tit*, etc., see Note.
> *Mab's-state*, Mab's chair of state.

The holy-water there is put:
A little brush of squirrel's hairs
(Composed of odd, not even pairs,)
Stands in the platter, or close by,
To purge the fairy family.
Near to the altar stands the priest,
There off'ring up the Holy Grist,
Ducking in mood and perfect tense,
With (much-good-do-'t him) reverence.
The altar is not here four-square,
Nor in a form triangular,
Nor made of glass, or wood, or stone,
But of a little transverse bone;
Which boys and bruckel'd children call
(Playing for points and pins) cockal.
Whose linen drapery is a thin
Subtile and ductile codlin's skin:
Which o'er the board is smoothly spread
With little seal-work damasked.
The fringe that circumbinds it too
Is spangle-work of trembling dew,
Which, gently gleaming, makes a show
Like frost-work glitt'ring on the snow.
Upon this fetuous board doth stand
Something for show-bread, and at hand,
Just in the middle of the altar,

Bruckel'd, begrimed.
Cockal, a game played with four huckle-bones.
Codlin, an apple.
Fetuous, feat, neat.

8

Upon an end, the fairy-psalter,
Grac'd with the trout-flies' curious wings,
Which serve for watchet ribbonings.
Now, we must know, the elves are led
Right by the rubric which they read.
And, if report of them be true,
They have their text for what they do;
Aye, and their book of canons too.
And, as Sir Thomas Parson tells,
They have their book of articles;
And, if that fairy-knight not lies,
They have their book of homilies;
And other scriptures that design
A short but righteous discipline.
The basin stands the board upon
To take the free oblation:
A little pin-dust, which they hold
More precious than we prize our gold
Which charity they give to many
Poor of the parish, if there's any.
Upon the ends of these neat rails,
Hatch'd with the silver-light of snails,
The elves in formal manner fix
Two pure and holy candlesticks:
In either which a small tall bent
Burns for the altar's ornament.
For sanctity they have to these

> *Watchet*, pale blue.
> *Hatch'd*, inlaid.
> *Bent*, bent grass.

Their curious copes and surplices
Of cleanest cobweb hanging by
In their religious vestery.
They have their ash-pans and their brooms
To purge the chapel and the rooms;
Their many mumbling Mass-priests here,
And many a dapper chorister,
Their ush'ring vergers,here likewise
Their canons and their chanteries.
Of cloister-monks they have enow,
Aye, and their abbey-lubbers too;
And, if their legend do not lie,
They much affect the papacy.
And since the last is dead, there's hope
Elf Boniface shall next be pope.
They have their cups and chalices;
Their pardons and indulgences;
Their beads of nits, bells, books, and wax
Candles, forsooth, and other knacks;
Their holy oil, their fasting spittle;
Their sacred salt here, not a little;
Dry chips, old shoes, rags, grease and bones;
Beside their fumigations
To drive the devil from the cod-piece
Of the friar (of work an odd piece).
Many a trifle, too, and trinket,
And for what use, scarce man would think it.
Next, then, upon the chanters' side
An apple's core is hung up dri'd,
With rattling kernels, which is rung
To call to morn and even-song.
            Nits, nuts.

The saint to which the most he prays
And offers incense nights and days,
The lady of the lobster is,
Whose foot-pace he doth stroke and kiss;
And humbly chives of saffron brings
For his most cheerful offerings.
When, after these, h'as paid his vows
He lowly to the altar bows;
And then he dons the silk-worm's shed,
Like a Turk's turban on his head,
And reverently departeth thence,
Hid in a cloud of frankincense,
And by the glow-worm's light well guided,
Goes to the feast that's now provided.

224. TO MISTRESS KATHERINE BRADSHAW, THE LOVELY, THAT CROWNED HIM WITH LAUREL.

MY muse in meads has spent her many hours,
Sitting, and sorting several sorts of flowers
To make for others garlands, and to set
On many a head here many a coronet;
But, amongst all encircled here, not one
Gave her a day of coronation,
Till you, sweet mistress, came and interwove
A laurel for her, ever young as love—
You first of all crown'd her: she must of due
Render for that a crown of life to you.

The lady of the lobster, part of the lobster's apparatus
for digestion.

     Foot-pace, a mat.   *Chives*, shreds.

225. THE PLAUDITE, OR END OF LIFE.

IF, after rude and boisterous seas,
My wearied pinnace here finds ease;
If so it be I've gained the shore
With safety of a faithful oar ;
If, having run my barque on ground,
Ye see the aged vessel crown'd :
What's to be done, but on the sands
Ye dance and sing and now clap hands ?
The first act's doubtful, but we say
It is the last commends the play.

226. TO THE MOST VIRTUOUS MISTRESS POT, WHO MANY TIMES ENTERTAINED HIM.

WHEN I through all my many poems look,
And see yourself to beautify my book,
Methinks that only lustre doth appear
A light fulfilling all the region here.
Gild still with flames this firmament, and be
A lamp eternal to my poetry.
Which, if it now or shall hereafter shine,
'Twas by your splendour, lady, not by mine.
The oil was yours ; and that I owe for yet :
He pays the half who does confess the debt.

227. TO MUSIC, TO BECALM HIS FEVER.

CHARM me asleep and melt me so
    With thy delicious numbers,
That, being ravished, hence I go
    Away in easy slumbers.

Ease my sick head
And make my bed,
Thou power that canst sever
From me this ill ;
And quickly still,
Though thou not kill,
My fever.

Thou sweetly canst convert the same
From a consuming fire
Into a gentle-licking flame,
And make it thus expire.
Then make me weep
My pains asleep ;
And give me such reposes
That I, poor I,
May think thereby
I live and die
'Mongst roses.

Fall on me like a silent dew,
Or like those maiden showers
Which, by the peep of day, do strew
A baptism o'er the flowers.
Melt, melt my pains
With thy soft strains ;
That, having ease me given,
With full delight
I leave this light,
And take my flight
For heaven.

228. UPON A GENTLEWOMAN WITH A SWEET VOICE.

So long you did not sing or touch your lute,
We knew 'twas flesh and blood that there sat mute.
But when your playing and your voice came in,
'Twas no more you then, but a cherubin.

229. UPON CUPID.

As lately I a garland bound,
'Mongst roses I there Cupid found;
I took him, put him in my cup,
And drunk with wine, I drank him up.
Hence then it is that my poor breast
Could never since find any rest.

230. UPON JULIA'S BREASTS.

DISPLAY thy breasts, my Julia—there let me
Behold that circummortal purity,
Between whose glories there my lips I'll lay,
Ravish'd in that fair *via lactea.*

231. BEST TO BE MERRY.

FOOLS are they who never know
How the times away do go;
But for us, who wisely see
Where the bounds of black death be,
Let's live merrily, and thus
Gratify the Genius.

Circummortal, more than mortal.

232. THE CHANGES TO CORINNA.

BE not proud, but now incline
Your soft ear to discipline.
You have changes in your life—
Sometimes peace and sometimes strife ;
You have ebbs of face and flows,
As your health or comes or goes ;
You have hopes, and doubts, and fears
Numberless, as are your hairs.
You have pulses that do beat
High, and passions less of heat.
You are young, but must be old,
And, to these, ye must be told
Time ere long will come and plough
Loathed furrows in your brow :
And the dimness of your eye
Will no other thing imply
    But you must die
    As well as I.

234. NEGLECT.

Art quickens nature ; care will make a face ;
Neglected beauty perisheth apace.

235. UPON HIMSELF.

MOP-EYED I am, as some have said,
Because I've lived so long a maid :
But grant that I should wedded be,

    Mop-eyed, shortsighted.

Should I a jot the better see?
No, I should think that marriage might,
Rather than mend, put out the light.

236. UPON A PHYSICIAN.

THOU cam'st to cure me, doctor, of my cold,
And caught'st thyself the more by twenty fold:
Prithee go home; and for thy credit be
First cured thyself, then come and cure me.

238. TO THE ROSE. A SONG.

Go, happy rose, and interwove
With other flowers, bind my love.
Tell her, too, she must not be
Longer flowing, longer free,
That so oft has fetter'd me.

Say, if she's fretful, I have bands
Of pearl and gold to bind her hands.
Tell her, if she struggle still,
I have myrtle rods (at will)
For to tame, though not to kill.

Take thou my blessing, thus, and go
And tell her this, but do not so,
Lest a handsome anger fly,
Like a lightning, from her eye,
And burn thee up as well as I.

240. TO HIS BOOK.

THOU art a plant sprung up to wither never,
But like a laurel to grow green for ever.

241. UPON A PAINTED GENTLEWOMAN.

MEN say y'are fair, and fair ye are, 'tis true;
But, hark! we praise the painter now, not you.

243. DRAW-GLOVES.

AT draw-gloves we'll play,
And prithee let's lay
A wager, and let it be this:
Who first to the sum
Of twenty shall come,
Shall have for his winning a kiss.

244. TO MUSIC, TO BECALM A SWEET-SICK YOUTH.

CHARMS, that call down the moon from out her
    sphere,
On this sick youth work your enchantments here:
Bind up his senses with your numbers so
As to entrance his pain, or cure his woe.
Fall gently, gently, and a while him keep
Lost in the civil wilderness of sleep:
That done, then let him, dispossessed of pain,
Like to a slumb'ring bride, awake again.

Draw-gloves, a game of talking by the fingers.

**245. TO THE HIGH AND NOBLE PRINCE GEORGE, DUKE,
MARQUIS, AND EARL OF BUCKINGHAM.**

NEVER my book's perfection did appear
Till I had got the name of Villars here :
Now 'tis so full that when therein I look
I see a cloud of glory fills my book.
Here stand it still to dignify our Muse,
Your sober handmaid, who doth wisely choose
Your name to be a laureate wreath to her
Who doth both love and fear you, honoured sir.

246. HIS RECANTATION.

LOVE, I recant,
And pardon crave
That lately I offended ;
But 'twas,
Alas !
To make a brave,
But no disdain intended.

No more I'll vaunt,
For now I see
Thou only hast the power
To find
And bind
A heart that's free,
And slave it in an hour.

247. THE COMING OF GOOD LUCK.

So good luck came, and on my roof did light,
Like noiseless snow, or as the dew of night :
Not all at once, but gently, as the trees
Are by the sunbeams tickled by degrees.

248. THE PRESENT; OR, THE BAG OF THE BEE.

FLY to my mistress, pretty pilfering bee,
And say thou bring'st this honey bag from me :
When on her lip thou hast thy sweet dew placed.
Mark if her tongue but slyly steal a taste.
If so, we live; if not, with mournful hum
Toll forth my death; next, to my burial come.

249. ON LOVE.

LOVE bade me ask a gift,
  And I no more did move
But this, that I might shift
  Still with my clothes my love:
That favour granted was;
  Since which, though I love many,
Yet so it comes to pass
  That long I love not any.

250. THE HOCK-CART OR HARVEST HOME. TO THE RIGHT HONOURABLE MILDMAY, EARL OF WESTMORELAND.

COME, sons of summer, by whose toil
We are the lords of wine and oil:
By whose tough labours and rough hands
We rip up first, then reap our lands.
Crowned with the ears of corn, now come,
And to the pipe sing harvest home.
Come forth, my lord, and see the cart
Dressed up with all the country art:
See here a maukin, there a sheet,
As spotless pure as it is sweet:
The horses, mares, and frisking fillies,
Clad all in linen white as lilies.
The harvest swains and wenches bound
For joy, to see the hock-cart crowned.
About the cart, hear how the rout
Of rural younglings raise the shout;
Pressing before, some coming after,
Those with a shout, and these with laughter.
Some bless the cart, some kiss the sheaves,
Some prank them up with oaken leaves:
Some cross the fill-horse, some with great
Devotion stroke the home-borne wheat:
While other rustics, less attent
To prayers than to merriment,
Run after with their breeches rent.
Well, on, brave boys, to your lord's hearth,

Maukin. a cloth.   *Fill-horse*, shaft-horse.

Glitt'ring with fire, where, for your mirth,
Ye shall see first the large and chief
Foundation of your feast, fat beef:
With upper stories, mutton, veal
And bacon (which makes full the meal),
With sev'ral dishes standing by,
As here a custard, there a pie,
And here all-tempting frumenty.
And for to make the merry cheer,
If smirking wine be wanting here,
There's that which drowns all care, stout beer;
Which freely drink to your lord's health,
Then to the plough, the commonwealth,
Next to your flails, your fans, your fats,
Then to the maids with wheaten hats:
To the rough sickle, and crook'd scythe,
Drink, frolic boys, till all be blithe.
Feed, and grow fat; and as ye eat
Be mindful that the lab'ring neat,
As you, may have their fill of meat.
And know, besides, ye must revoke
The patient ox unto the yoke,
And all go back unto the plough
And harrow, though they're hanged up now.
And, you must know, your lord's word's true,
Feed him ye must, whose food fills you;
And that this pleasure is like rain,
Not sent ye for to drown your pain,
But for to make it spring again.

Frumenty, wheat boiled in milk.
Fats, vats.

251. THE PERFUME.

To-morrow, Julia, I betimes must rise,
For some small fault to offer sacrifice:
The altar's ready: fire to consume
The fat; breathe thou, and there's the rich perfume.

252. UPON HER VOICE.

Let but thy voice engender with the string,
And angels will be born while thou dost sing.

253. NOT TO LOVE.

He that will not love must be
My scholar, and learn this of me:
There be in love as many fears
As the summer's corn has ears:
Sighs, and sobs, and sorrows more
Than the sand that makes the shore:
Freezing cold and fiery heats,
Fainting swoons and deadly sweats;
Now an ague, then a fever,
Both tormenting lovers ever.
Would'st thou know, besides all these,
How hard a woman 'tis to please,
How cross, how sullen, and how soon
She shifts and changes like the moon.
How false, how hollow she's in heart:
And how she is her own least part:
How high she's priz'd, and worth but small;
Little thou'lt love, or not at all.

254. TO MUSIC. A SONG.

MUSIC, thou queen of heaven, care-charming spell,
    That strik'st a stillness into hell :
Thou that tam'st tigers, and fierce storms that rise,
    With thy soul-melting lullabies,
Fall down, down, down from those thy chiming
      spheres,
To charm our souls, as thou enchant'st our ears.

255. TO THE WESTERN WIND.

SWEET western wind, whose luck it is,
    Made rival with the air,
To give Perenna's lip a kiss,
    And fan her wanton hair.

Bring me but one, I'll promise thee,
    Instead of common showers,
Thy wings shall be embalm'd by me,
    And all beset with flowers.

256. UPON THE DEATH OF HIS SPARROW.
AN ELEGY.

WHY do not all fresh maids appear
To work love's sampler only here,
Where spring-time smiles throughout the year
Are not here rosebuds, pinks, all flowers
Nature begets by th' sun and showers,
Met in one hearse-cloth to o'erspread
The body of the under-dead ?

Phil, the late dead, the late dead dear,
O! may no eye distil a tear
For you once lost, who weep not here!
Had Lesbia, too-too kind, but known
This sparrow, she had scorn'd her own:
And for this dead which under lies
Wept out her heart, as well as eyes.
But, endless peace, sit here and keep
My Phil the time' he has to sleep;
And thousand virgins come and weep
To make these flowery carpets show
Fresh as their blood, and ever grow,
Till passengers shall spend their doom:
Not Virgil's gnat had such a tomb.

257. TO PRIMROSES FILLED WITH MORNING DEW.

WHY do ye weep, sweet babes? can tears
    Speak grief in you,
    Who were but born
    Just as the modest morn
    Teem'd her refreshing dew?
Alas! you have not known that shower
    That mars a flower,
    Nor felt th' unkind
    Breath of a blasting wind,

Phil, otherwise Philip or Phip, was a pet name for a sparrow.

Virgil's gnat, the *Culex* attributed to Virgil.

9

Nor are ye worn with years,
   Or warp'd as we,
Who think it strange to see
Such pretty flowers, like to orphans young,
To speak by tears before ye have a tongue.

Speak, whimp'ring younglings, and make known
         The reason why
         Ye droop and weep;
      Is it for want of sleep?
      Or childish lullaby?
Or that ye have not seen as yet
         The violet?
      Or brought a kiss
From that sweetheart to this?
No, no, this sorrow shown
         By your tears shed
Would have this lecture read:
That things of greatest, so of meanest worth,
Conceiv'd with grief are, and with tears brought forth.

258. HOW ROSES CAME RED.

Roses at first were white,
   Till they could not agree,
Whether my Sappho's breast
   Or they more white should be.

But, being vanquish'd quite,
   A blush their cheeks bespread;
Since which, believe the rest,
   The roses first came red.

259. COMFORT TO A LADY UPON THE DEATH OF
HER HUSBAND.

Dry your sweet cheek, long drown'd with sorrow's
  rain,
Since, clouds dispers'd, suns gild the air again.
Seas chafe and fret, and beat, and overboil,
But turn soon after calm as balm or oil.
Winds have their time to rage; but when they cease
The leafy trees nod in a still-born peace.
Your storm is over; lady, now appear
Like to the peeping springtime of the year.
Off then with grave clothes; put fresh colours on,
And flow and flame in your vermilion.
Upon your cheek sat icicles awhile;
Now let the rose reign like a queen, and smile.

260. HOW VIOLETS CAME BLUE.

Love on a day, wise poets tell,
  Some time in wrangling spent,
Whether the violets should excel,
  Or she, in sweetest scent.

But Venus having lost the day,
  Poor girls, she fell on you:
And beat ye so, as some dare say,
  Her blows did make ye blue.

262. TO THE WILLOW-TREE.

THOU art to all lost love the best,
  The only true plant found,
Wherewith young men and maids distres't,
  And left of love, are crown'd.

When once the lover's rose is dead,
  Or laid aside forlorn :
Then willow-garlands 'bout the head
  Bedew'd with tears are worn.

When with neglect, the lovers' bane,
  Poor maids rewarded be,
For their love lost, their only gain
  · Is but a wreath from thee.

And underneath thy cooling shade,
  When weary of the light,
The love-spent youth and love-sick maid
  Come to weep out the night.

263. MRS. ELIZ. WHEELER, UNDER THE NAME OF
THE LOST SHEPHERDESS.

AMONG the myrtles as I walk'd,
Love and my sighs thus intertalk'd :
Tell me, said I, in deep distress,
Where I may find my shepherdess.
Thou fool, said Love, know'st thou not this?
In everything that's sweet she is.

In yond' carnation go and seek,
There thou shalt find her lip and cheek:
In that enamell'd pansy by,
There thou shalt have her curious eye:
In bloom of peach and rose's bud,
There waves the streamer of her blood.
'Tis true, said I, and thereupon
I went to pluck them one by one,
To make of parts a union :
But on a sudden all were gone.
At which I stopp'd; said Love, these be
The true resemblances of thee ;
For, as these flowers, thy joys must die,
And in the turning of an eye :
And all thy hopes of her must wither,
Like those short sweets, ere knit together.

264. TO THE KING.

IF when these lyrics, Cæsar, you shall hear,
And that Apollo shall so touch your ear
As for to make this, that, or any one,
Number your own, by free adoption ;
That verse, of all the verses here, shall be
The heir to this *great realm of poetry.*

265. TO THE QUEEN.

Goddess of youth, and lady of the spring,
Most fit to be the consort to a king,
Be pleas'd to rest you in this sacred grove
Beset with myrtles, whose each leaf drops love.

Many a sweet-fac'd wood-nymph here is seen,
Of which chaste order you are now the queen:
Witness their homage when they come and strew
Your walks with flowers, and give their crowns to
 you.
Your leafy throne, with lily-work possess,
And be both princess here and poetess.

266. THE POET'S GOOD WISHES FOR THE MOST HOPEFUL AND HANDSOME PRINCE, THE DUKE OF YORK.

MAY his pretty dukeship grow
Like t'a rose of Jericho:
Sweeter far than ever yet
Showers or sunshines could beget.
May the Graces and the Hours
Strew his hopes and him with flowers:
And so dress him up with love
As to be the chick of Jove.
May the thrice-three sisters sing
Him the sovereign of their spring:
And entitle none to be
Prince of Helicon but he.
May his soft foot, where it treads,
Gardens thence produce and meads:
And those meadows full be set
With the rose and violet.
May his ample name be known
To the last succession:
And his actions high be told
Through the world, but writ in gold.

267. TO ANTHEA, WHO MAY COMMAND HIM
ANYTHING.

BID me to live, and I will live
   Thy Protestant to be,
Or bid me love, and I will give
   A loving heart to thee.

A heart as soft, a heart as kind,
   A heart as sound and free
As in the whole world thou canst find,
   That heart I'll give to thee.

Bid that heart stay, and it will stay
   To honour thy decree:
Or bid it languish quite away,
   And't shall do so for thee.

Bid me to weep, and I will weep
   While I have eyes to see:
And, having none, yet I will keep
   A heart to weep for thee.

Bid me despair, and I'll despair
   Under that cypress-tree:
Or bid me die, and I will dare
   E'en death to die for thee.

Thou art my life, my love, my heart,
   The very eyes of me:
And hast command of every part
   To live and die for thee.

268. PREVISION OR PROVISION.

That prince takes soon enough the victor's room
Who first provides not to be overcome.

269. OBEDIENCE IN SUBJECTS.

The gods to kings the judgment give to sway:
The subjects only glory to obey.

270. MORE POTENT, LESS PECCANT.

He that may sin, sins least: leave to transgress
Enfeebles much the seeds of wickedness.

271. UPON A MAID THAT DIED THE DAY SHE WAS MARRIED.

THAT morn which saw me made a bride,
The evening witness'd that I died.
Those holy lights, wherewith they guide
Unto the bed the bashful bride,
Serv'd but as tapers for to burn
And light my relics to their urn.
This epitaph, which here you see,
Supplied the epithalamy.

274. TO MEADOWS.

YE have been fresh and green,
  Ye have been fill'd with flowers,
And ye the walks have been
  Where maids have spent their hours.

You have beheld how they
　　With wicker arks did come
To kiss and bear away
　　The richer cowslips home.

Y'ave heard them sweetly sing,
　　And seen them in a round :
Each virgin like a spring,
　　With honeysuckles crown'd.

But now we see none here
　　Whose silvery feet did tread,
And with dishevell'd hair
　　Adorn'd this smoother mead.

Like unthrifts, having spent
　　Your stock and needy grown,
Y'are left here to lament
　　Your poor estates, alone.

275. CROSSES.

THOUGH goods things answer many good intents,
Crosses do still bring forth the best events.

276. MISERIES.

THOUGH hourly comforts from the gods we see,
No life is yet life-proof from misery.

Round, a rustic dance.

278. TO HIS HOUSEHOLD GODS.

RISE, household gods, and let us go ;
But whither I myself not know.
First, let us dwell on rudest seas ;
Next, with severest savages ;
Last, let us make our best abode
Where human foot as yet ne'er trod :
Search worlds of ice, and rather there
Dwell than in loathed Devonshire.

279. TO THE NIGHTINGALE AND ROBIN REDBREAST.

WHEN I departed am, ring thou my knell,
Thou pitiful and pretty Philomel :
And when I'm laid out for a corse, then be
Thou sexton, redbreast, for to cover me.

280. TO THE YEW AND CYPRESS TO GRACE HIS FUNERAL.

BOTH you two have
Relation to the grave :
And where
The funeral-trump sounds, you are there,

I shall be made,
Ere long, a fleeting shade :
Pray, come
And do some honour to my tomb.

Do not deny
My last request ; for I
Will be
Thankful to you, or friends, for me.

281. I CALL AND I CALL.

I CALL, I call: who do ye call?
The maids to catch this cowslip ball:
But since these cowslips fading be,
Troth, leave the flowers, and, maids, take me.
Yet, if that neither you will do,
Speak but the word and I'll take you.

282. ON A PERFUMED LADY.

You say you're sweet; how should we know
Whether that you be sweet or no?
From powders and perfumes keep free,
Then we shall smell how sweet you be.

283. A NUPTIAL SONG OR EPITHALAMY ON SIR CLIPSEBY CREW AND HIS LADY.

WHAT's that we see from far? the spring of day
Bloom'd from the east, or fair enjewell'd May
    Blown out of April, or some new
    Star filled with glory to our view,
       Reaching at heaven,
To add a nobler planet to the seven?
    Say, or do we not descry
Some goddess in a cloud of tiffany
      To move, or rather the
    Emergent Venus from the sea?

Tiffany, gauze.

'Tis she! 'tis she! or else some more divine
Enlightened substance; mark how from the shrine
  Of holy saints she paces on,
   Treading upon vermilion
    And amber: spic-
ing the chaft air with fumes of Paradise.
   Then come on, come on and yield
A savour like unto a blessed field
    When the bedabbled morn
  Washes the golden ears of corn.

See where she comes; and smell how all the street
Breathes vineyards and pomegranates: O how sweet!
  As a fir'd altar is each stone,
  Perspiring pounded cinnamon.
    The phœnix' nest,
Built up of odours, burneth in her breast.
   Who, therein, would not consume
His soul to ash-heaps in that rich perfume?
    Bestroking fate the while
  He burns to embers on the pile.

Hymen, O Hymen! tread the sacred ground;
Show thy white feet and head with marjoram
   crown'd:
  Mount up thy flames and let thy torch
  Display the bridegroom in the porch,
    In his desires
More towering, more disparkling than thy fires:

  More disparkling, more widespreading.

Show her how his eyes do turn
And roll about, and in their motions burn
   Their balls to cinders: haste
 Or else to ashes he will waste.

Glide by the banks of virgins, then, and pass
The showers of roses, lucky four-leav'd grass:
  The while the cloud of younglings sing
 And drown ye with a flowery spring;
   While some repeat
Your praise and bless you, sprinkling you with
  wheat;
  While that others do divine,
Bless'd is the bride on whom the sun doth shine;
   And thousands gladly wish
 You multiply as doth a fish.

And, beauteous bride, we do confess y'are wise
In dealing forth these bashful jealousies:
  In love's name do so; and a price
 Set on yourself by being nice:
   But yet take heed;
What now you seem be not the same indeed,
 And turn apostate: love will,
Part of the way be met or sit stone-still.
   On, then, and though you slow-
 ly go, yet, howsoever, go.

And now y'are entered; see the coddled cook
Runs from his torrid zone to pry and look

   Nice, fastidious.
   Coddled, lit. boiled.

And bless his dainty mistress : see
The aged point out, " This is she
　　　Who now must sway
The house (love shield her) with her yea and nay " :
　　And the smirk butler thinks it
　　Sin in's napery not to express his wit ;
　　　　　Each striving to devise
Some gin wherewith to catch your eyes.

To bed, to bed, kind turtles, now, and write
This the short'st day, and this the longest night ;
　　　But yet too short for you : 'tis we
　　　Who count this night as long as three,
　　　　　Lying alone,
Telling the clock strike ten, eleven, twelve, one.
　　　Quickly, quickly then prepare,
And let the young men and the bride-maids share
　　　　　Your garters ; and their joints
　　Encircle with the bridegroom's points.

By the bride's eyes, and by the teeming life
Of her green hopes, we charge ye that no strife
　　(Farther than gentleness tends) gets place
　　Among ye, striving for her lace :　　　　　•
　　　　　O do not fall
Foul in these noble pastimes, lest ye call
　　Discord in, and so divide
The youthful bridegroom and the fragrant bride :
　　　　　Which love forfend ; but spoken
　　Be't to your praise, no peace was broken.

Lace, girdle.

Strip her of springtime, tender-whimpering maids,
Now autumn's come, when all these flowery aids
    Of her delays must end; dispose
    That lady-smock, that pansy, and that rose
        Neatly apart,
But for prick-madam and for gentle-heart,
    And soft maidens'-blush, the bride
Makes holy these, all others lay aside :
        Then strip her, or unto her
    Let him come who dares undo her.

And to enchant ye more, see everywhere
About the roof a siren in a sphere,
    As we think, singing to the din
    Of many a warbling cherubin.
        O mark ye how
The soul of nature melts in numbers : now
    See, a thousand Cupids fly
To light their tapers at the bride's bright eye.
        To bed, or her they'll tire,
    Were she an element of fire.

And to your more bewitching, see, the proud
Plump bed bear up, and swelling like a cloud,
    Tempting the two too modest ; can
    Ye see it brusle like a swan,
        And you be cold
To meet it when it woos and seems to fold
    The arms to hug it ?   Throw, throw
Yourselves into the mighty overflow
        Of that white pride, and drown
    The night with you in floods of down.

    Brusle, raise its feathers.

The bed is ready, and the maze of love
Looks for the treaders ; everywhere is wove
  Wit and new mystery ; read, and
  Put in practice, to understand
    And know each wile,
Each hieroglyphic of a kiss or smile ;
  And do it to the full ; reach
High in your own conceit, and some way teach
    Nature and art one more
  Play than they ever knew before.

If needs we must for ceremony's sake,
Bless a sack-posset, luck go with it, take
  The night-charm quickly, you have spells
  And magics for to end, and hells
    To pass ; but such
And of such torture as no one would grutch
  To live therein for ever : fry
And consume, and grow again to die
    And live, and, in that case,
  Love the confusion of the place.

But since it must be done, despatch, and sew
Up in a sheet your bride, and what if so
  It be with rock or walls of brass
  Ye tower her up, as Danae was ;

    Grutch, grumble.

Think you that this
Or hell itself a powerful bulwark is ?
　　I tell ye no ; but like a
Bold bolt of thunder he will make his way,
　　　　And rend the cloud, and throw
　　The sheet about like flakes of snow.

All now is hushed in silence : midwife-moon
With all her owl-eyed issue begs a boon,
　　Which you must grant ; that's entrance ; with
　　Which extract, all we can call pith
　　　　And quintessence
Of planetary bodies, so commence,
　　All fair constellations
Looking upon ye, that two nations,
　　　　Springing from two such fires
　　May blaze the virtue of their sires.

284. THE SILKEN SNAKE.

For sport my Julia threw a lace
Of silk and silver at my face :
Watchet the silk was, and did make
A show as if 't had been a snake :
The suddenness did me afright,
But though it scar'd, it did not bite.

Lace, a girdle.
Watchet, pale blue.
10

285. UPON HIMSELF.

I AM sieve-like, and can hold
Nothing hot or nothing cold.
Put in love, and put in too
Jealousy, and both will through:
Put in fear, and hope, and doubt;
What comes in runs quickly out:
Put in secrecies withal,
Whate'er enters, out it shall:
But if you can stop the sieve,
For mine own part, I'd as lief
Maids should say or virgins sing,
Herrick keeps, as holds nothing.

286. UPON LOVE.

LOVE's a thing, as I do hear,
Ever full of pensive fear;
Rather than to which I'll fall,
Trust me, I'll not like at all.
If to love I should intend,
Let my hair then stand an end:
And that terror likewise prove
Fatal to me in my love.
But if horror cannot slake
Flames which would an entrance make
Then the next thing I desire
Is, to love and live i' th' fire.

An end, on end.

287. REVERENCE TO RICHES.

LIKE to the income must be our expense;
Man's fortune must be had in reverence.

288. DEVOTION MAKES THE DEITY.

Who forms a godhead out of gold or stone
Makes not a god, but he that prays to one.

289. TO ALL YOUNG MEN THAT LOVE.

I COULD wish you all who love,
That ye could your thoughts remove
From your mistresses, and be
Wisely wanton, like to me,
I could wish you dispossessed
Of that *fiend that mars your rest,*
And with tapers comes to fright
Your weak senses in the night.
I could wish ye all who fry
Cold as ice, or cool as I ;
But if flames best like ye, then,
Much good do 't ye, gentlemen.
I a merry heart will keep,
While you wring your hands and weep.

290. THE EYES.

'TIS a known principle in war,
The eyes be first that conquered are.

291. NO FAULT IN WOMEN.

No fault in women to refuse
The offer which they most would choose.
No fault in women to confess
How tedious they are in their dress.
No fault in women to lay on
The tincture of vermilion :
And there to give the cheek a dye
Of white, where nature doth deny.
No fault in women to make show
Of largeness when they're nothing so :
(When true it is the outside swells
With inward buckram, little else).
No fault in women, though they be
But seldom from suspicion free.
No fault in womankind at all
If they but slip and never fall.

293. OBERON'S FEAST.

Shapcot ! to thee the fairy state
I, with discretion, dedicate.
Because thou prizest things that are
Curious and unfamiliar.
Take first the feast ; these dishes gone,
We'll see the Fairy Court anon.

A LITTLE mushroom table spread,
After short prayers, they set on bread ;
A moon-parch'd grain of purest wheat,
With some small glittering grit to eat

His choice bits with; then in a trice
They make a feast less great than nice.
But all this while his eye is serv'd,
We must not think his ear was sterv'd;
But that there was in place to stir
His spleen, the chirring grasshopper,
The merry cricket, puling fly,
The piping gnat for minstrelsy.
And now we must imagine, first,
The elves present, to quench his thirst,
A pure seed-pearl of infant dew
Brought and besweetened in a blue
And pregnant violet; which done,
His kitling eyes begin to run
Quite through the table, where he spies
The horns of papery butterflies:
Of which he eats, and tastes a little
Of that we call the cuckoo's spittle.
A little fuzz-ball pudding stands
By, yet not blessed by his hands;
That was too coarse: but then forthwith
He ventures boldly on the pith
Of sugar'd rush, and eats the sagg
And well-bestrutted bee's sweet bag:
Gladding his palate with some store
Of emmets' eggs; what would he more?
But beards of mice, a newt's stewed thigh,
A bloated earwig and a fly;

> *Sagg*, laden.
> *Bestrutted*, swollen.

With the red-capp'd worm that's shut
Within the concave of a nut,
Brown as his tooth.   A little moth
Late fatten'd in a piece of cloth :
With withered cherries, mandrakes' ears,
Moles' eyes ; to these the slain stag's tears
The unctuous dewlaps of a snail,
The broke-heart of a nightingale
O'ercome in music ; with a wine
Ne'er ravish'd from the flattering vine,
But gently press'd from the soft side
Of the most sweet and dainty bride,
Brought in a dainty daisy, which
He fully quaffs up to bewitch
His blood to height ; this done, commended
Grace by his priest ; *the feast is ended.*

294. EVENT OF THINGS NOT IN OUR POWER.

By time and counsel do the best we can,
Th' event is never in the power of man.

295. UPON HER BLUSH.

WHEN Julia blushes she does show
Cheeks like to roses when they blow.

296. MERITS MAKE THE MAN.

OUR honours and our commendations be
Due to the merits, not authority.

297. TO VIRGINS.

HEAR, ye virgins, and I'll teach
What the times of old did preach.
Rosamond was in a bower
Kept, as Danae in a tower:
But yet Love, who subtle is,
Crept to that, and came to this.
Be ye lock'd up like to these,
Or the rich Hesperides,
Or those babies in your eyes,
In their crystal nunneries;
Notwithstanding Love will win,
Or else force a passage in:
And as coy be as you can,
Gifts will get ye, or the man.

298. VIRTUE.

EACH must in virtue strive for to excel;
That man lives twice that lives the first life well.

299. THE BELLMAN.

FROM noise of scare-fires rest ye free,
From murders *Benedicite.*
From all mischances that may fright
Your pleasing slumbers in the night,
Mercy secure ye all, and keep
The goblin from ye while ye sleep.
Past one o'clock, and almost two!
My masters all, good-day to you.

Babies in your eyes, see Note to p. 17.
Scare-fires, alarms of fire.

300. BASHFULNESS.

OF all our parts, the eyes express
The sweetest kind of bashfulness.

301. TO THE MOST ACCOMPLISHED GENTLEMAN, MASTER EDWARD NORGATE, CLERK OF THE SIGNET TO HIS MAJESTY. EPIG.

FOR one so rarely tun'd to fit all parts,
For one to whom espous'd are all the arts,
Long have I sought for, but could never see
Them all concentr'd in one man, but thee.
Thus, thou that man art whom the fates conspir'd
To make but one, and that's thyself, admir'd.

302. UPON PRUDENCE BALDWIN: HER SICKNESS.

PRUE, my dearest maid, is sick,
Almost to be lunatic:
Æsculapius! come and bring
Means for her recovering;
And a gallant cock shall be
Offer'd up by her to thee.

303. TO APOLLO. A SHORT HYMN.

PHŒBUS! when that I a verse
Or some numbers more rehearse,

Cock, the traditional offering to Æsculapius; cp. the
last words of Socrates; cp. Ben Jonson, Epig. xiii.

Tune my words that they may fall
Each way smoothly musical:
For which favour there shall be
Swans devoted unto thee.

304. A HYMN TO BACCHUS.

BACCHUS, let me drink no more;
Wild are seas that want a shore.
When our drinking has no stint,
There is no one pleasure in't.
I have drank up, for to please
Thee, that great cup Hercules:
Urge no more, and there shall be
Daffodils given up to thee.

306. ON HIMSELF.

HERE down my wearied limbs I'll lay;
My pilgrim's staff, my weed of gray,
My palmer's hat, my scallop's shell,
My cross, my cord, and all, farewell.
For having now my journey done,
Just at the setting of the sun,
Here I have found a chamber fit,
God and good friends be thanked for it,
Where if I can a lodger be,
A little while from tramplers free,
At my up-rising next I shall,
If not requite, yet thank ye all.
Meanwhile, the holy-rood hence fright
The fouler fiend and evil sprite
From scaring you or yours this night.

307. CASUALTIES.

GOOD things that come of course, far less do please
Than those which come by sweet contingencies.

308. BRIBES AND GIFTS GET ALL.

DEAD falls the cause if once the hand be mute ;
But let that speak, the client gets the suit.

309. THE END.

IF well thou hast begun, go on fore-right ;
It is the end that crowns us, not the fight.

310. UPON A CHILD THAT DIED.

HERE she lies, a pretty bud,
Lately made of flesh and blood :
Who as soon fell fast asleep
As her little eyes did peep.
Give her strewings, but not stir
The earth that lightly covers her.

312. CONTENT, NOT CATES.

TIS not the food, but the content
That makes the table's merriment.
Where trouble serves the board, we eat
The platters there as soon as meat.
A little pipkin with a bit
Of mutton or of veal in it,
Set on my table, trouble-free,
More than a feast contenteth me.

313. THE ENTERTAINMENT ; OR, PORCH-VERSE, AT
THE MARRIAGE OF MR. HENRY NORTHLY AND
THE MOST WITTY MRS. LETTICE YARD.

WELCOME ! but yet no entrance, till we bless
First you, then you, and both for white success.
Profane no porch, young man and maid, for fear
Ye wrong the Threshold-god that keeps peace here :
Please him, and then all good-luck will betide
You, the brisk bridegroom, you, the dainty bride.
Do all things sweetly, and in comely wise ;
Put on your garlands first, then sacrifice :
That done, when both of you have seemly fed,
We'll call on Night, to bring ye both to bed :
Where, being laid, all fair signs looking on,
Fish-like, increase then to a million ;
And millions of spring-times may ye have,
Which spent, one death bring to ye both one grave.

314. THE GOOD-NIGHT OR BLESSING.

BLESSINGS in abundance come
To the bride and to her groom ;
May the bed and this short night
Know the fulness of delight !
Pleasures many here attend ye,
And, ere long, a boy Love send ye
Curled and comely, and so trim,
Maids, in time, may ravish him.
Thus a dew of graces fall
On ye both ; good-night to all.

316. TO DAFFODILS.

FAIR daffodils, we weep to see
   You haste away so soon;
As yet the early-rising sun
   Has not attain'd his noon.
     Stay, stay,
    Until the hasting day
      Has run
    But to the evensong;
And, having prayed together, we
   Will go with you along.

We have short time to stay, as you,
   We have as short a spring;
As quick a growth to meet decay,
   As you, or anything.
     We die,
    As your hours do, and dry
      Away,
    Like to the summer's rain;
Or as the pearls of morning's dew,
   Ne'er to be found again.

318. UPON A LADY THAT DIED IN CHILD-BED, AND LEFT A DAUGHTER BEHIND HER.

As gilliflowers do but stay
To blow, and seed, and so away;
So you, sweet lady, sweet as May,
The garden's glory, lived a while
To lend the world your scent and smile.

But when your own fair print was set
Once in a virgin flosculet,
Sweet as yourself, and newly blown,
To give that life, resigned your own :
But so as still the mother's power
Lives in the pretty lady-flower.

319. A NEW-YEAR'S GIFT SENT TO SIR SIMON STEWARD.

No news of navies burnt at seas;
No noise of late-spawn'd tittyries;
No closet plot, or open vent,
That frights men with a parliament;
No new device or late-found trick
To read by the stars the kingdom's sick;
No gin to catch the state, or wring
The freeborn nostril of the king,
We send to you; but here a jolly
Verse, crown'd with ivy and with holly,
That tells of winter's tales and mirth,
That milkmaids make about the hearth,
Of Christmas sports, the wassail-bowl,
That['s] tost up, after fox-i'-th'-hole;
Of blind-man-buff, and of the care
That young men have to shoe the mare;
Of Twelfth-tide cakes, of peas and beans,
Wherewith you make those merry scenes,

Tittyries, *i.e.*, the Tityre-tues; see Note.
Fox-i'-th'-hole, a game of hopping.
To shoe the mare, or, shoe the wild mare, a Christmas
game.

Whenas ye choose your king and queen,
And cry out: *Hey, for our town green;*
Of ash-heaps, in the which ye use
Husbands and wives by streaks to choose;
Of crackling laurel, which fore-sounds
A plenteous harvest to your grounds:
Of these and such-like things for shift,
We send instead of New-Year's gift.
Read then, and when your faces shine
With buxom meat and cap'ring wine,
Remember us in cups full crown'd,
And let our city-health go round,
Quite through the young maids and the men,
To the ninth number, if not ten;
Until the fired chesnuts leap
For joy to see the fruits ye reap
From the plump chalice and the cup,
That tempts till it be tossed up;
Then as ye sit about your embers,
Call not to mind those fled Decembers,
But think on these that are t' appear
As daughters to the instant year:
Sit crown'd with rosebuds, and carouse
Till Liber Pater twirls the house
About your ears; and lay upon
The year your cares that's fled and gone.
And let the russet swains the plough
And harrow hang up, resting now;

Buxom, tender.
Liber Pater, Father Bacchus.

And to the bagpipe all address,
Till sleep takes place of weariness.
And thus, throughout, with Christmas plays
Frolic the full twelve holidays.

320. MATINS; OR, MORNING PRAYER.

WHEN with the virgin morning thou dost rise,
Crossing thyself, come thus to sacrifice;
First wash thy heart in innocence, then bring
Pure hands, pure habits, pure, pure everything.
Next to the altar humbly kneel, and thence
Give up thy soul in clouds of frankincense.
Thy golden censers, fill'd with odours sweet,
Shall make thy actions with their ends to meet.

321. EVENSONG.

BEGIN with Jove; then is the work half done,
And runs most smoothly when 'tis well begun.
Jove's is the first and last: the morn's his due,
The midst is thine; but Jove's the evening too;
As sure a matins does to him belong,
So sure he lays claim to the evensong.

322. THE BRACELET TO JULIA.

WHY I tie about thy wrist,
    Julia, this my silken twist;
    For what other reason is't,
But to show thee how, in part,

Thou my pretty captive art?
But thy bondslave is my heart;
'Tis but silk that bindeth thee,
Knap the thread and thou art free:
But 'tis otherwise with me;
I am bound, and fast bound, so
That from thee I cannot go;
If I could, I would not so.

323. THE CHRISTIAN MILITANT.

A MAN prepar'd against all ills to come,
That dares to dead the fire of martyrdom;
That sleeps at home, and sailing there at ease,
Fears not the fierce sedition of the seas;
That's counter-proof against the farm's mishaps,
Undreadful too of courtly thunderclaps;
That wears one face, like heaven, and never shows
A change when fortune either comes or goes;
That keeps his own strong guard in the despite
Of what can hurt by day or harm by night;
That takes and re-delivers every stroke
Of chance (as made up all of rock and oak);
That sighs at others' death, smiles at his own
Most dire and horrid crucifixion.
Who for true glory suffers thus, we grant
Him to be here our Christian militant.

324. A SHORT HYMN TO LAR.

THOUGH I cannot give thee fires
Glittering to my free desires;
These accept, and I'll be free,
Offering poppy unto thee.

325. ANOTHER TO NEPTUNE.

MIGHTY Neptune, may it please
Thee, the rector of the seas,
That my barque may safely run
Through thy watery region;
And a tunny-fish shall be
Offered up with thanks to thee.

327. HIS EMBALMING TO JULIA.

FOR my embalming, Julia, do but this;
Give thou my lips but their supremest kiss,
Or else transfuse thy breath into the chest
Where my small relics must for ever rest;
That breath the balm, the myrrh, the nard shall
  be,
To give an incorruption unto me.

328. GOLD BEFORE GOODNESS.

How rich a man is all desire to know;
But none inquires if good he be or no.

329. THE KISS. A DIALOGUE.

1. Among thy fancies tell me this,
   What is the thing we call a kiss?
2. I shall resolve ye what it is.

   It is a creature born and bred
   Between the lips (all cherry-red),
   By love and warm desires fed.
Chor. And makes more soft the bridal bed.

2. It is an active flame that flies,
   First, to the babies of the eyes;
   And charms them there with lullabies.
Chor. And stills the bride, too, when she cries.

2. Then to the chin, the cheek, the ear,
   It frisks and flies, now here, now there,
   'Tis now far off, and then 'tis near.
Chor. And here and there and everywhere.

1. Has it a speaking virtue? 2. Yes.
1. How speaks it, say? 2. Do you but this;
   Part your joined lips, then speaks your kiss
Chor. And this love's sweetest language is.

1. Has it a body? 2. Aye, and wings
   With thousand rare encolourings;
   And, as it flies, it gently sings,
Chor. Love honey yields, but never stings.

330. THE ADMONITION.

Seest thou those diamonds which she wears
    In that rich carcanet;
Or those, on her dishevell'd hairs,
    Fair pearls in order set?
Believe, young man, all those were tears
    By wretched wooers sent,
In mournful hyacinths and rue,
    That figure discontent;
Which when not warmed by her view,
    By cold neglect, each one
Congeal'd to pearl and stone;
    Which precious spoils upon her
    She wears as trophies of her honour.
Ah then, consider, what all this implies:
She that will wear thy tears would wear thine eyes.

331. TO HIS HONOURED KINSMAN, SIR WILLIAM SOAME. EPIG.

I can but name thee, and methinks I call
All that have been, or are canonical
For love and bounty to come near, and see
Their many virtues volum'd up in thee;
In thee, brave man! whose incorrupted fame
Casts forth a light like to a virgin flame;
And as it shines it throws a scent about,
As when a rainbow in perfumes goes out.
So vanish hence, but leave a name as sweet
As benjamin and storax when they meet.

Carcanet, necklace.   *Benjamin*, gum benzoin.
Storax or *Styrax*, another resinous gum.

332. ON HIMSELF.

Ask me why I do not sing
To the tension of the string
As I did not long ago,
When my numbers full did flow?
Grief, ay, me! hath struck my lute
And my tongue, at one time, mute.

333. TO LAR.

No more shall I, since I am driven hence,
Devote to thee my grains of frankincense;
No more shall I from mantle-trees hang down,
To honour thee, my little parsley crown;
No more shall I (I fear me) to thee bring
My chives of garlic for an offering;
No more shall I from henceforth hear a choir
Of merry crickets by my country fire.
Go where I will, thou lucky Lar stay here,
Warm by a glitt'ring chimney all the year.

334. THE DEPARTURE OF THE GOOD DEMON.

What can I do in poetry
Now the good spirit's gone from me?
Why, nothing now but lonely sit
And over-read what I have writ.

Chives, shreds.

335. CLEMENCY.

For punishment in war it will suffice
If the chief author of the faction dies;
Let but few smart, but strike a fear through all;
Where the fault springs there let the judgment fall.

336. HIS AGE, DEDICATED TO HIS PECULIAR FRIEND, M. JOHN WICKES, UNDER THE NAME OF POSTHUMUS.

Ah Posthumus! our years hence fly,
And leave no sound; nor piety,
  Or prayers, or vow
Can keep the wrinkle from the brow;
  But we must on,
As fate does lead or draw us; none,
None, Posthumus, could ere decline
The doom of cruel Proserpine.

The pleasing wife, the house, the ground,
Must all be left, no one plant found
  To follow thee,
Save only the curs'd cypress tree;
  A merry mind
Looks forward, scorns what's left behind;
Let's live, my Wickes, then, while we may,
And here enjoy our holiday.

W'ave seen the past best times, and these
Will ne'er return; we see the seas

Posthumus, the name is taken from Horace, Ode ii.
14, from which the beginning of this lyric is translated.

And moons to wane
But they fill up their ebbs again ;
        But vanish'd man,
Like to a lily lost, ne'er can,
Ne'er can repullulate, or bring
His days to see a second spring.

But on we must, and thither tend,
Where Anchus and rich Tullus blend
        Their sacred seed :
Thus has infernal Jove decreed ;
        We must be made,
Ere long a song, ere long a shade.
Why then, since life to us is short,
Let's make it full up by our sport.

Crown we our heads with roses then,
And 'noint with Tyrian balm ; for when
        We two are dead,
The world with us is buried.
        Then live we free
As is the air, and let us be
Our own fair wind, and mark each one
Day with the white and lucky stone.

We are not poor, although we have
No roofs of cedar, nor our brave

Repullulate, be born again.

Anchus and rich Tullus. Herrick is again translating
from Horace (Ode iv. 7, 14).

Baiæ, nor keep
Account of such a flock of sheep;
Nor bullocks fed
To lard the shambles: barbels bred
To kiss our hands; nor do we wish
For Pollio's lampreys in our dish.

If we can meet and so confer
Both by a shining salt-cellar,
And have our roof,
Although not arch'd, yet weather-proof,
And ceiling free
From that cheap candle bawdery;
We'll eat our bean with that full mirth
As we were lords of all the earth.

Well then, on what seas we are toss'd,
Our comfort is, we can't be lost.
Let the winds drive
Our barque, yet she will keep alive
Amidst the deeps.
'Tis constancy, my Wickes, which keeps
The pinnace up; which, though she errs
I' th' seas, she saves her passengers.

Baiæ, the favourite sea-side resort of the Romans in the time of Horace.

Pollio, Vedius Pollio, who fed his lampreys with human flesh. *Ob.*, B.C. 15.

Bawdery, dirt (with no moral meaning).

Say, we must part (sweet mercy bless
Us both i' th' sea, camp, wilderness),
          Can we so far
Stray to become less circular
          Than we are now?
No, no, that self-same heart, that vow
Which made us one, shall ne'er undo,
Or ravel so to make us two.

Live in thy peace; as for myself,
When I am bruised on the shelf
          Of time, and show
My locks behung with frost and snow;
          When with the rheum,
The cough, the ptisick, I consume
Unto an almost nothing; then
The ages fled I'll call again,

And with a tear compare these last
Lame and bad times with those are past;
          While Baucis by,
My old lean wife, shall kiss it dry.
          And so we'll sit
By th' fire, foretelling snow and sleet,
And weather by our aches, grown '
Now old enough to be our own

True calendars, as puss's ear
Washed o'er's, to tell what change is near:

Circular, self-sufficing, the "in se ipso totus teres
atque rotundus" of Horace.   Sat. ii. 7, 86.

Then to assuage
The gripings of the chine by age,
I'll call my young
Iülus to sing such a song
I made upon my Julia's breast;
And of her blush at such a feast.

Then shall he read that flower of mine,
Enclos'd within a crystal shrine;
A primrose next;
A piece, then, of a higher text,
For to beget
In me a more transcendent heat
Than that insinuating fire,
Which crept into each aged sire,

When the fair Helen, from her eyes,
Shot forth her loving sorceries;
At which I'll rear
Mine aged limbs above my chair,
And, hearing it,
Flutter and crow as in a fit
Of fresh concupiscence, and cry:
No lust there's like to poetry.

Thus, frantic-crazy man, God wot,
I'll call to mind things half-forgot,
And oft between
Repeat the times that I have seen !
Thus ripe with tears,
And twisting my Iülus' hairs,

Iülus, the son of Æneas.

Doting, I'll weep and say, in truth,
Baucis, these were my sins of youth.

Then next I'll cause my hopeful lad,
If a wild apple can be had,
　　　　To crown the hearth,
Lar thus conspiring with our mirth;
　　　　Then to infuse
Our browner ale into the cruse,
Which sweetly spic'd, we'll first carouse
Unto the Genius of the house.

Then the next health to friends of mine,
Loving the brave Burgundian wine,
　　　　High sons of pith,
Whose fortunes I have frolicked with;
　　　　Such as could well
Bear up the magic bough and spell;
And dancing 'bout the mystic thyrse,
Give up the just applause to verse:

To those, and then again to thee,
We'll drink, my Wickes, until we be
　　　　Plump as the cherry,
Though not so fresh, yet full as merry
　　　　As the cricket,
The untam'd heifer, or the pricket,
Until our tongues shall tell our ears
We're younger by a score of years.

　　Pith, marrow.
　　Thyrse, bacchic staff.
　　Pricket, a buck in his second year.

Thus, till we see the fire less shine
From th' embers than the kitling's eyne,
     We'll still sit up,
Sphering about the wassail-cup
     To all those times
Which gave me honour for my rhymes.
The coal once spent, we'll then to bed,
Far more than night-bewearied.

337. A SHORT HYMN TO VENUS.

GODDESS, I do love a girl,
Ruby-lipp'd and tooth'd with pearl;
If so be I may but prove
Lucky in this maid I love,
I will promise there shall be
Myrtles offer'd up to thee.

338. TO A GENTLEWOMAN ON JUST DEALING.

TRUE to yourself and sheets, you'll have me swear;
You shall, if righteous dealing I find there.
Do not you fall through frailty; I'll be sure
To keep my bond still free from forfeiture.

339. THE HAND AND TONGUE.

Two parts of us successively command:
The tongue in peace; but then in war the hand.

340. UPON A DELAYING LADY.

COME, come away,
Or let me go;
Must I here stay
Because y'are slow,
And will continue so?
Troth, lady, no.

I scorn to be
A slave to state:
And, since I'm free,
I will not wait
Henceforth at such a rate
For needy fate.

If you desire
My spark should glow,
The peeping fire
You must blow,
Or I shall quickly grow
To frost or snow.

341. TO THE LADY MARY VILLARS, GOVERNESS TO THE PRINCESS HENRIETTA.

WHEN I of Villars do but hear the name,
It calls to mind that mighty Buckingham,
Who was your brave exalted uncle here,
Binding the wheel of fortune to his sphere,
Who spurned at envy, and could bring with ease
An end to all his stately purposes.

For his love then, whose sacred relics show
Their resurrection and their growth in you;
And for my sake, who ever did prefer
You above all those sweets of Westminster;
Permit my book to have a free access
To kiss your hand, most dainty governess.

342. UPON HIS JULIA.

WILL ye hear what I can say
Briefly of my Julia?
Black and rolling is her eye,
Double-chinn'd and forehead high;
Lips she has all ruby red,
Cheeks like cream enclareted;
And a nose that is the grace
And proscenium of her face.
So that we may guess by these
The other parts will richly please.

343. TO FLOWERS.

IN time of life I graced ye with my verse;
Do now your flowery honours to my hearse.
You shall not languish, trust me; virgins here
Weeping shall make ye flourish all the year.

344. TO MY ILL READER.

THOU say'st my lines are hard,
And I the truth will tell—
They are both hard and marr'd
If thou not read'st them well.

345. THE POWER IN THE PEOPLE.

LET kings command and do the best they may,
The saucy subjects still will bear the sway.

346. A HYMN TO VENUS AND CUPID.

SEA-BORN goddess, let me be
By thy son thus grac'd and thee;
That whene'er I woo, I find
Virgins coy but not unkind.   .
Let me when I kiss a maid
Taste her lips so overlaid
With love's syrup, that I may,
In your temple when I pray,
Kiss the altar and confess
There's in love no bitterness.

347. ON JULIA'S PICTURE.

How am I ravish'd! when I do but see
The painter's art in thy sciography?
If so, how much more shall I dote thereon
When once he gives it incarnation?

348. HER BED.

SEE'ST thou that cloud as silver clear,
Plump, soft, and swelling everywhere?
'Tis Julia's bed, and she sleeps there.

Sciography, the profile or section of a building.

349. HER LEGS.

FAIN would I kiss my Julia's dainty leg,
Which is as white and hairless as an egg.

350. UPON HER ALMS.

SEE how the poor do waiting stand
For the expansion of thy hand.
A wafer dol'd by thee will swell
Thousands to feed by miracle.

351. REWARDS.

STILL to our gains our chief respect is had ;
Reward it is that makes us good or bad.

352. NOTHING NEW.

NOTHING is new; we walk where others went ·
There's no vice now but has his precedent.

353. THE RAINBOW.

LOOK how the rainbow doth appear
But in one only hemisphere ;
So likewise after our decease
No more is seen the arch of peace.
That cov'nant's here, the under-bow,
That nothing shoots but war and woe.

354. THE MEADOW-VERSE; OR, ANNIVERSARY TO MISTRESS BRIDGET LOWMAN.

COME with the spring-time forth, fair maid, and be
This year again the meadow's deity.
Yet ere ye enter give us leave to set
Upon your head this flowery coronet;
To make this neat distinction from the rest,
You are the prime and princess of the feast;
To which with silver feet lead you the way,
While sweet-breath nymphs attend on you this day.
This is your hour, and best you may command,
Since you are lady of this fairy land.
Full mirth wait on you, and such mirth as shall
Cherish the cheek but make none blush at all.

355. THE PARTING VERSE, THE FEAST THERE ENDED.

LOTH to depart, but yet at last each one
Back must now go to's habitation;
Not knowing thus much when we once do sever,
Whether or no that we shall meet here ever.
As for myself, since time a thousand cares
And griefs hath filed upon my silver hairs,
'Tis to be doubted whether I next year
Or no shall give ye a re-meeting here.
If die I must, then my last vow shall be,
You'll with a tear or two remember me,

Meadow-verse, to be recited at a rustic feast.

Your sometime poet; but if fates do give
Me longer date and more fresh springs to live,
Oft as your field shall her old age renew,
Herrick shall make the meadow-verse for you.

356. UPON JUDITH. EPIG.

JUDITH has cast her old skin and got new,
And walks fresh varnish'd to the public view;
Foul Judith was and foul she will be known
For all this fair transfiguration.

359. TO THE RIGHT HONOURABLE PHILIP, EARL OF PEMBROKE AND MONTGOMERY.

How dull and dead are books that cannot show
A prince of Pembroke, and that Pembroke you!
You who are high born, and a lord no less
Free by your fate than fortune's mightiness,
Who hug our poems, honour'd sir, and then
The paper gild and laureate the pen.
Nor suffer you the poets to sit cold,
But warm their wits and turn their lines to gold.
Others there be who righteously will swear
Those smooth-paced numbers amble everywhere,
And these brave measures go a stately trot;
Love those, like these, regard, reward them not.
But you, my lord, are one whose hand along
Goes with your mouth or does outrun your tongue;
Paying before you praise, and, cockering wit,
Give both the gold and garland unto it.

Cockering, pampering.

360. AN HYMN TO JUNO.

STATELY goddess, do thou please,
Who are chief at marriages,
But to dress the bridal bed
When my love and I shall wed;
And a peacock proud shall be
Offered up by us to thee.

362. UPON SAPPHO SWEETLY PLAYING AND SWEETLY SINGING.

WHEN thou dost play and sweetly sing—
Whether it be the voice or string
Or both of them that do agree
Thus to entrance and ravish me—
This, this I know, I'm oft struck mute,
And die away upon thy lute.

364. CHOP-CHERRY.

THOU gav'st me leave to kiss,
Thou gav'st me leave to woo;
Thou mad'st me think, by this
And that, thou lov'dst me too.

But I shall ne'er forget
How, for to make thee merry,
Thou mad'st me chop, but yet
Another snapp'd the cherry.

Chop-cherry, another name of cherry-bob.

365. TO THE MOST LEARNED, WISE, AND ARCH-ANTIQUARY, M. JOHN SELDEN.

I, WHO have favour'd many, come to be
Grac'd now, at last, or glorified by thee,
Lo! I, the lyric prophet, who have set
On many a head the delphic coronet,
Come unto thee for laurel, having spent
My wreaths on those who little gave or lent.
Give me the daphne, that the world may know it,
Whom they neglected thou hast crown'd a poet.
A city here of heroes I have made
Upon the rock whose firm foundation laid,
Shall never shrink; where, making thine abode,
Live thou a Selden, that's a demi-god.

366. UPON HIMSELF.

THOU shalt not all die; for, while love's fire shines
Upon his altar, men shall read thy lines,
And learn'd musicians shall, to honour Herrick's
Fame and his name, both set and sing his lyrics.

367. UPON WRINKLES.

WRINKLES no more are or no less
Than beauty turned to sourness.

Daphne, i.e., the laurel

370. PRAY AND PROSPER.

FIRST offer incense, then thy field and meads
Shall smile and smell the better by thy beads.
The spangling dew, dredg'd o'er the grass, shall be
Turn'd all to mell and manna there for thee.
Butter of amber, cream, and wine, and oil
Shall run, as rivers, all throughout thy soil.
Would'st thou to sincere silver turn thy mould?
Pray once, twice pray, and turn thy ground to gold.

371. HIS LACHRYMÆ; OR, MIRTH TURNED TO MOURNING.

CALL me no more,
As heretofore,
The music of a feast;
Since now, alas!
The mirth that was
In me is dead or ceas'd.

Before I went,
To banishment,
Into the loathed west,
I could rehearse
A lyric verse,
And speak it with the best.

But time, ay me!
Has laid, I see,

Beads, prayers.
Mell, honey.
Sincere silver, pure silver.

My organ fast asleep,
   And turn'd my voice
   Into the noise
Of those that sit and weep.

375. TO THE MOST FAIR AND LOVELY MISTRESS ANNE SOAME, NOW LADY ABDIE.

So smell those odours that do rise
From out the wealthy spiceries ;
So smells the flower of blooming clove,
Or roses smother'd in the stove ;
So smells the air of spiced wine,
Or essences of jessamine ;
So smells the breath about the hives
When well the work of honey thrives,
And all the busy factors come
Laden with wax and honey home ;
So smell those neat and woven bowers
All over-arch'd with orange flowers,
And almond blossoms that do mix
To make rich these aromatics ;
So smell those bracelets and those bands
Of amber chaf'd between the hands,
When thus enkindled they transpire
A noble perfume from the fire ;
The wine of cherries, and to these
The cooling breath of respasses ;

     Factors, workers.
     Respasses, raspberries.

The smell of morning's milk and cream,
Butter of cowslips mix'd with them;
Of roasted warden or bak'd pear,
These are not to be reckon'd here,
Whenas the meanest part of her,
Smells like the maiden pomander.
Thus sweet she smells, or what can be
More lik'd by her or lov'd by me.

376. UPON HIS KINSWOMAN, MISTRESS ELIZABETH HERRICK.

SWEET virgin, that I do not set
The pillars up of weeping jet
Or mournful marble, let thy shade
Not wrathful seem, or fright the maid
Who hither at her wonted hours
Shall come to strew thy earth with flowers.
No; know, bless'd maid, when there's not one
Remainder left of brass or stone,
Thy living epitaph shall be,
Though lost in them, yet found in me;
Dear, in thy bed of roses then,
Till this world shall dissolve as men,
Sleep while we hide thee from the light,
Drawing thy curtains round: Good-night.

Pomander, ball of scent.

377. A PANEGYRIC TO SIR LEWIS PEMBERTON.

TILL I shall come again let this suffice,
    I send my salt, my sacrifice
To thee, thy lady, younglings, and as far
    As to thy Genius and thy Lar;
To the worn threshold, porch, hall, parlour, kitchen,
    The fat-fed smoking temple, which in
The wholesome savour of thy mighty chines
    Invites to supper him who dines,
Where laden spits, warp'd with large ribs of beef,
    Not represent but give relief
To the lank stranger and the sour swain,
    Where both may feed and come again;
For no black-bearded vigil from thy door
    Beats with a button'd-staff the poor;
But from thy warm love-hatching gates each may
    Take friendly morsels and there stay
To sun his thin-clad members if he likes,
    For thou no porter keep'st who strikes.
No comer to thy roof his guest-rite wants,
    Or staying there is scourg'd with taunts
Of some rough groom, who, yirkt with corns, says:
      " Sir,
    Y'ave dipped too long i' th' vinegar;
And with our broth, and bread, and bits, sir friend.
    Y'ave fared well: pray make an end;

Vigil, watchman.
Button'd-staff, staff with a knob at its end.
Yirkt, scourged.

Two days y'ave larded here; a third, ye know,
    Makes guests and fish smell strong; pray
        go
You to some other chimney, and there take
    Essay of other giblets; make
Merry at another's hearth—y'are here
    Welcome as thunder to our beer;
Manners know distance, and a man unrude
    Would soon recoil and not intrude
His stomach to a second meal". No, no!
    Thy house well fed and taught can show
No such crabb'd vizard: thou hast learnt thy train
    With heart and hand to entertain,
And by the armsful, with a breast unhid,
    As the old race of mankind did,
When either's heart and either's hand did strive
    To be the nearer relative.
Thou dost redeem those times, and what was lost
    Of ancient honesty may boast
It keeps a growth in thee, and so will run
    A course in thy fame's pledge, thy son.
Thus, like a Roman tribune, thou thy gate
    Early sets ope to feast and late;
Keeping no currish waiter to affright
    With blasting eye the appetite,
Which fain would waste upon thy cates, but that
    The trencher-creature marketh what
Best and more suppling piece he cuts, and by
    Some private pinch tells danger's nigh

> *Redeem*, buy back.
> *Suppling*, tender.

A hand too desp'rate, or a knife that bites
    Skin-deep into the pork, or lights
Upon some part of kid, as if mistook,
    When checked by the butler's look.
No, no; thy bread, thy wine, thy jocund beer
    Is not reserved for Trebius here,
But all who at thy table seated are
    Find equal freedom, equal fare;
And thou, like to that hospitable god,
    Jove, joy'st when guests make their abode
To eat thy bullock's thighs, thy veals, thy fat
    Wethers, and never grudged at.
The *pheasant, partridge, gotwit, reeve, ruff, rail,*
    The *cock,* the *curlew* and the *quail,*
These and thy choicest viands do extend
    Their taste unto the lower end
Of thy glad table: not a dish more known
    To thee than unto anyone.
But as thy meat so thy *immortal wine*
    Makes the smirk face of each to shine
And spring fresh rosebuds, while the salt, the wit,
    Flows from the wine and graces it;
While reverence, waiting at the bashful board,
    Honours my lady and my lord.
No scurril jest; no open scene is laid
    Here for to make the face afraid;
But temperate mirth dealt forth, and so discreet-
    ly that it makes the meat more sweet;
And adds perfumes unto the wine, which thou
    Dost rather pour forth than allow

Trebius, friend of the epicure Lucullus; cp. Juv. v. 19.

By cruse and measure; thus devoting wine
  As the Canary Isles were thine;
But with that wisdom and that method, as
  No one that's there his guilty glass
Drinks of distemper, or has cause to cry
  Repentance to his liberty.
No, thou knowest order, ethics, and has read
  All economics, know'st to lead
A house-dance neatly, and canst truly show
  How far a figure ought to go,
Forward or backward, sideward, and what pace
  Can give, and what retract a grace;
What gesture, courtship, comeliness agrees
  With those thy primitive decrees,
To give subsistence to thy house, and proof
  What Genii support thy roof,
Goodness and Greatness; not the oaken piles;
  For these and marbles have their whiles
To last, but not their ever; virtue's hand
  It is which builds 'gainst fate to stand.
Such is thy house, whose firm foundation's trust
  Is more in thee than in her dust
Or depth; these last may yield and yearly
  shrink
  When what is strongly built, no chink
Or yawning rupture can the same devour,
  But fix'd it stands, by her own power
And well-laid bottom, on the iron and rock
  Which tries and counter-stands the shock
And ram of time, and by vexation grows
  The stronger; *virtue dies when foes*

Are wanting to her exercise, but great
      And large she spreads by dust and sweat.
Safe stand thy walls and thee, and so both will,
      Since neither's height was rais'd by th' ill
Of others; since no stud, no stone, no piece
      Was rear'd up by the poor man's fleece;
No widow's tenement was rack'd to gild
      Or fret thy ceiling or to build
A sweating-closet to anoint the silk-
      soft skin, or bathe in asses' milk;
No orphan's pittance left him serv'd to set
      The pillars up of lasting jet,
For which their cries might beat against thine ears,
      Or in the damp jet read their tears.
No plank from hallowed altar does appeal
      To yond' Star-Chamber, or does seal
A curse to thee or thine; but all things even
      Make for thy peace and pace to heaven.
Go on directly so, as just men may
      A thousand times more swear than say:
This is that princely Pemberton who can
      Teach man to keep a god in man;
And when wise poets shall search out to see
      Good men, they find them all in thee.

378. TO HIS VALENTINE ON ST. VALENTINE'S DAY.

OFT have I heard both youths and virgins say
Birds choose their mates, and couple too this day;
But by their flight I never can divine
When I shall couple with my valentine.

382. UPON M. BEN. JONSON. EPIG.

AFTER the rare arch-poet, Jonson, died,
The sock grew loathsome, and the buskin's pride,
Together with the stage's glory, stood
Each like a poor and pitied widowhood.
The cirque profan'd was, and all postures rack'd;
For men did strut, and stride, and stare, not act.
Then temper flew from words, and men did squeak,
Look red, and blow, and bluster, but not speak;
No holy rage or frantic fires did stir
Or flash about the spacious theatre.
No clap of hands, or shout, or praise's proof
Did crack the play-house sides, or cleave her roof.
Artless the scene was, and that monstrous sin
Of deep and arrant ignorance came in:
Such ignorance as theirs was who once hiss'd
At thy unequall'd play, the *Alchemist;*
Oh, fie upon 'em!   Lastly, too, all wit
In utter darkness did, and still will sit,
Sleeping the luckless age out, till that she
Her resurrection has again with thee.

383. ANOTHER.

THOU had'st the wreath before, now take the tree,
That henceforth none be laurel-crown'd but thee.

384. TO HIS NEPHEW, TO BE PROSPEROUS IN HIS ART OF PAINTING.

ON, as thou hast begun, brave youth, and get
The palm from Urbin, Titian, Tintoret,

Urbin, Raphael.

Brugel and Coxu, and the works outdo
Of Holbein and that mighty Rubens too.
So draw and paint as none may do the like,
No, not the glory of the world, Vandyke.

386. A VOW TO MARS.

STORE of courage to me grant,
Now I'm turn'd a combatant;
Help me, so that I my shield,
Fighting, lose not in the field.
That's the greatest shame of all
That in warfare can befall.
Do but this, and there shall be
Offer'd up a wolf to thee.

387. TO HIS MAID, PREW.

THESE summer-birds did with thy master stay
The times of warmth, but then they flew away,
Leaving their poet, being now grown old,
Expos'd to all the coming winter's cold.
But thou, kind Prew, did'st with my fates abide
As well the winter's as the summer's tide;
For which thy love, live with thy master here,
Not one, but all the seasons of the year.

Brugel, Jan Breughel, Dutch landscape painter (1569-1625), or his father or brother.

Coxu, Michael van Coxcie, Flemish painter (1497-1592).

388. A CANTICLE TO APOLLO.

PLAY, Phœbus, on thy lute;
And we will all sit mute,
By listening to thy lyre,
That sets all ears on fire.

Hark, hark, the god does play!
And as he leads the way
Through heaven the very spheres,
As men, turn all to ears.

389. A JUST MAN.

A JUST man's like a rock that turns the wrath
Of all the raging waves into a froth.

390. UPON A HOARSE SINGER.

SING me to death; for till thy voice be clear,
'Twill never please the palate of mine ear.

391. HOW PANSIES OR HEART'S-EASE CAME FIRST.

FROLIC virgins once these were,
Over-loving, living here;
Being here their ends denied,
Ran for sweethearts mad, and died.
Love, in pity of their tears,
And their loss in blooming years,
For their restless here-spent hours,
Gave them heart's-ease turn'd to flowers.

392. TO HIS PECULIAR FRIEND, SIR EDWARD FISH, KNIGHT BARONET.

SINCE, for thy full deserts, with all the rest
Of these chaste spirits that are here possest
Of life eternal, time has made thee one
For growth in this my rich plantation,
Live here ; but know 'twas virtue, and not chance,
That gave thee this so high inheritance.
Keep it for ever, grounded with the good,
Who hold fast here an endless livelihood.

393. LAR'S PORTION AND THE POET'S PART.

AT my homely country-seat
I have there a little wheat,
Which I work to meal, and make.
Therewithal a holy cake:
Part of which I give to Lar,
Part is my peculiar.

394. UPON MAN.

MAN is compos'd here of a twofold part:
The first of nature, and the next of art:
Art presupposes nature ; nature she
Prepares the way for man's docility.

Peculiar, his own property.

395. LIBERTY.

THOSE ills that mortal men endure
So long, are capable of cure,
As they of freedom may be sure;
But, that denied, a grief, though small,
Shakes the whole roof, or ruins all.

396. LOTS TO BE LIKED.

LEARN this of me, where'er thy lot doth fall,
Short lot or not, to be content with all.

397. GRIEFS.

JOVE may afford us thousands of reliefs,
Since man expos'd is to a world of griefs.

399. THE DREAM.

By dream I saw one of the three
Sisters of fate appear to me;
Close to my bedside she did stand,
Showing me there a firebrand;
She told me too, as that did spend,
So drew my life unto an end.
Three quarters were consum'd of it;
Only remained a little bit,
Which will be burnt up by-and-by;
Then, Julia, weep, for I must die.

402. CLOTHES DO BUT CHEAT AND COZEN US.

Away with silks, away with lawn,
I'll have no scenes or curtains drawn;
Give me my mistress as she is,
Dress'd in her nak'd simplicities;
For as my heart e'en so mine eye
Is won with flesh, not drapery.

403. TO DIANEME.

Show me thy feet; show me thy legs, thy thighs;
Show me those fleshy principalities;
Show me that hill where smiling love doth sit.
Having a living fountain under it;
Show me thy waist, then let me therewithal,
By the assention of thy lawn, see all.

404. UPON ELECTRA.

When out of bed my love doth spring,
'Tis but as day a-kindling;
But when she's up and fully dress'd,
'Tis then broad day throughout the east

405. TO HIS BOOK.

Have I not blest thee? Then go forth, nor fear
Or spice, or fish, or fire, or close-stools here.
But with thy fair fates leading thee, go on
With thy most white predestination.

13

Nor think these ages that do hoarsely sing
The farting tanner and familiar king,
The dancing friar, tatter'd in the bush;
Those monstrous lies of little Robin Rush,
Tom Chipperfeild, and pretty lisping Ned,
That doted on a maid of gingerbread;
The flying pilchard and the frisking dace,
With all the rabble of Tim Trundell's race
(Bred from the dunghills and adulterous rhymes),
Shall live, and thou not superlast all times.
No, no; thy stars have destin'd thee to see
The whole world die and turn to dust with thee.
He's greedy of his life who will not fall
Whenas a public ruin bears down all.

406. OF LOVE.

I DO not love, nor can it be
Love will in vain spend shafts on me;
I did this godhead once defy,
Since which I freeze, but cannot fry.
Yet out, alas! the death's the same,
Kill'd by a frost or by a flame.

407. UPON HIMSELF.

I DISLIK'D but even now;
Now I love I know not how.
Was I idle, and that while
Was I fir'd with a smile?
I'll to work, or pray; and then
I shall quite dislike again.

The farting tanner, etc., see Note.

408. ANOTHER.

Love he that will, it best likes me
To have my neck from love's yoke free.

412. THE MAD MAID'S SONG.

Good-morrow to the day so fair.
  Good-morning, sir, to you;
Good-morrow to mine own torn hair,
  Bedabbled with the dew.

Good-morning to this primrose too,
  Good-morrow to each maid
That will with flowers the tomb bestrew
  Wherein my love is laid.

Ah! woe is me, woe, woe is me,
  Alack and well-a-day!
For pity, sir, find out that bee
  Which bore my love away.

I'll seek him in your bonnet brave,
  I'll seek him in your eyes;
Nay, now I think th'ave made his grave
  I' th' bed of strawberries.

I'll seek him there; I know ere this
  The cold, cold earth doth shake him;
But I will go or send a kiss
  By you, sir, to awake him.

Pray, hurt him not; though he be dead,
  He knows well who do love him,
And who with green turfs rear his head,
  And who do rudely move him.

He's soft and tender (pray take heed);
  With bands of cowslips bind him,
And bring him home; but 'tis decreed
  That I shall never find him.

413. TO SPRINGS AND FOUNTAINS.

I HEARD ye could cool heat, and came
With hope you would allay the same;
Thrice I have wash'd but feel no cold,
Nor find that true which was foretold.
Methinks, like mine, your pulses beat
And labour with unequal heat;
Cure, cure yourselves, for I descry
Ye boil with love as well as I.

414. UPON JULIA'S UNLACING HERSELF.

TELL if thou canst, and truly, whence doth come
This camphor, storax, spikenard, galbanum;
These musks, these ambers, and those other smells,
Sweet as the vestry of the oracles:
I'll tell thee: while my Julia did unlace
Her silken bodice but a breathing space,
The passive air such odour then assum'd,
As when to Jove great Juno goes perfum'd,
Whose pure immortal body doth transmit
A scent that fills both heaven and earth with it.

415. TO BACCHUS, A CANTICLE.

WHITHER dost thou whorry me,
Bacchus, being full of thee?
This way, that way, that way, this,
Here and there a fresh love is.
That doth like me, this doth please,
Thus a thousand mistresses
I have now; yet I alone,
Having all, enjoy not one.

416. THE LAWN.

WOULD I see lawn, clear as the heaven, and thin?
It should be only in my Julia's skin,
Which so betrays her blood as we discover
The blush of cherries when a lawn's cast over.

417. THE FRANKINCENSE.

WHEN my off'ring next I make,
Be thy hand the hallowed cake,
And thy breast the altar whence
Love may smell the frankincense.

420. TO SYCAMORES.

I'M sick of love, O let me lie
Under your shades to sleep or die!
Either is welcome, so I have
Or here my bed, or here my grave.

Whorry, carry rapidly.

Why do you sigh, and sob, and keep
Time with the tears that I do weep?
Say, have ye sense, or do you prove
What crucifixions are in love?
I know ye do, and that's the why
You sigh for love as well as I.

421. A PASTORAL SUNG TO THE KING:

MONTANO, SILVIO, AND MIRTILLO, SHEPHERDS.

Mon. BAD are the times. *Sil.* And worse than
  they are we.

Mon. Troth, bad are both; worse fruit and ill the
  tree:
The feast of shepherds fail. *Sil.* None crowns the
  cup
Of wassail now or sets the quintell up;
And he who us'd to lead the country-round,
Youthful Mirtillo, here he comes grief-drown'd.

Ambo. Let's cheer him up. *Sil.* Behold him
  weeping-ripe.

Mir. Ah! Amaryllis, farewell mirth and pipe;
Since thou art gone, no more I mean to play
To these smooth lawns my mirthful roundelay.
Dear Amaryllis! *Mon.* Hark! *Sil.* Mark! *Mir.*
  This earth grew sweet
Where, Amaryllis, thou didst set thy feet.

Ambo. Poor pitied youth! *Mir.* And here the
  breath of kine
And sheep grew more sweet by that breath of thine.

Quintell, quintain or tilting board.

This flock of wool and this rich lock of hair,
This ball of cowslips, these she gave me here.

  Sil. Words sweet as love itself. Montano, hark !

  Mir. This way she came, and this way too she
    went ;

How each thing smells divinely redolent !
Like to a field of beans when newly blown,
Or like a meadow being lately mown.

  Mon. A sweet-sad passion ——

  Mir. In dewy mornings when she came this way
Sweet bents would bow to give my love the day ;
And when at night she folded had her sheep,
Daisies would shut, and, closing, sigh and weep.
Besides (ay me !) since she went hence to dwell,
The voices' daughter ne'er spake syllable.
But she is gone. *Sil.* Mirtillo, tell us whither.

  Mir. Where she and I shall never meet together.

  Mon. Forfend it Pan, and, Pales, do thou please
To give an end. *Mir.* To what ? *Sil.* Such griefs
    as these.

  Mir. Never, O never ! Still I may endure
The wound I suffer, never find a cure.

  Mon. Love for thy sake will bring her to these hills
And dales again. *Mir.* No, I will languish still ;
And all the while my part shall be to weep,
And with my sighs, call home my bleating sheep :
And in the rind of every comely tree
I'll carve thy name, and in that name kiss thee.

     Bents, grasses.
     Pales, the goddess of sheepfolds.

Mon. Set with the sun thy woes.　*Sil.* The day
　　grows old,
And time it is our full-fed flocks to fold.
　Chor. The shades grow great, but greater grows
　　our sorrow;
　　　　　　　But let's go steep
　　　　　　　Our eyes in sleep,
　　　　　　　And meet to weep
　　　　　　　　　To-morrow.

422. THE POET LOVES A MISTRESS, BUT NOT TO MARRY.

　　　　　I DO not love to wed,
　　　　　Though I do like to woo;
　　　　　And for a maidenhead
　　　　　I'll beg and buy it too.

　　　　　I'll praise and I'll approve
　　　　　Those maids that never vary;
　　　　　And fervently I'll love,
　　　　　But yet I would not marry.

　　　　　I'll hug, I'll kiss, I'll play,
　　　　　And, cock-like, hens I'll tread,
　　　　　And sport it any way
　　　　　But in the bridal bed.

　　　　　For why? that man is poor
　　　　　Who hath but one of many,
　　　　　But crown'd he is with store
　　　　　That, single, may have any.

Why then, say, what is he,
To freedom so unknown,
Who, having two or three,
Will be content with one?

425. THE WILLOW GARLAND.

A WILLOW garland thou did'st send
   Perfum'd, last day, to me,
Which did but only this portend—
   I was forsook by thee.

Since so it is, I'll tell thee what,
   To-morrow thou shalt see
Me wear the willow; after that,
   To die upon the tree.

As beasts unto the altars go
   With garlands dress'd, so I
Will, with my willow-wreath, also
   Come forth and sweetly die.

427. A HYMN TO SIR CLIPSEBY CREW.

   'TWAS not love's dart,
   Or any blow
   Of want, or foe,
   Did wound my heart
With an eternal smart;

   But only you,
   My sometimes known

Companion,
My dearest Crew,
That me unkindly slew.

May your fault die,
And have no name
In books of fame;
Or let it lie
Forgotten now, as I.

We parted are
And now no more,
As heretofore,
By jocund Lar
Shall be familiar.

But though we sever,
My Crew shall see
That I will be
Here faithless never,
But love my Clipseby ever.

430. EMPIRES.

EMPIRES of kings are now, and ever were,
As Sallust saith, coincident to fear.

431. FELICITY QUICK OF FLIGHT.

EVERY time seems short to be
That's measured by felicity;
But one half-hour that's made up here
With grief, seems longer than a year.

436. THE CROWD AND COMPANY.

In holy meetings there a man may be
One of the crowd, not of the company.

438. POLICY IN PRINCES.

That princes may possess a surer seat,
'Tis fit they make no one with them too great.

440. UPON THE NIPPLES OF JULIA'S BREAST.

Have ye beheld (with much delight)
A red rose peeping through a white?
Or else a cherry, double grac'd,
Within a lily centre plac'd?
Or ever mark'd the pretty beam
A strawberry shows half-drown'd in cream?
Or seen rich rubies blushing through
A pure smooth pearl and orient too?
So like to this, nay all the rest,
Is each neat niplet of her breast.

441. TO DAISIES, NOT TO SHUT SO SOON.

Shut not so soon; the dull-ey'd night
   Has not as yet begun
To make a seizure on the light,
   Or to seal up the sun.

No marigolds yet closed are,
   No shadows great appear;

Nor doth the early shepherd's star
  Shine like a spangle here.

Stay but till my Julia close
  Her life-begetting eye,
And let the whole world then dispose
  Itself to live or die.

442. TO THE LITTLE SPINNERS.

YE pretty housewives, would ye know
The work that I would put ye to?
This, this it should be: for to spin
A lawn for me, so fine and thin
As it might serve me for my skin.
For cruel Love has me so whipp'd
That of my skin I all am stripp'd;
And shall despair that any art
Can ease the rawness or the smart,
Unless you skin again each part.
Which mercy if you will but do,
I call all maids to witness to
What here I promise: that no broom
Shall now or ever after come
To wrong a spinner or her loom.

444. OBERON'S PALACE.

AFTER the feast, my Shapcot, see
The fairy court I give to thee;

Spinners, spiders.

Where we'll present our Oberon, led
Half-tipsy to the fairy bed,
Where Mab he finds, who there doth lie,
Not without mickle majesty.
Which done, and thence remov'd the light,
We'll wish both them and thee good-night.

Full as a bee with thyme, and red
As cherry harvest, now high fed
For lust and action, on he'll go
To lie with Mab, though all say no.
Lust has no ears ; he's sharp as thorn,
And fretful, carries hay in's horn,
And lightning in his eyes ; and flings
Among the elves, if moved, the stings
Of peltish wasps ; well know his guard—
Kings, though they're hated, will be fear'd.
Wine lead[s] him on.   Thus to a grove,
Sometimes devoted unto love,
Tinselled with twilight, he and they,
Led by the shine of snails, a way
Beat with their num'rous feet, which, by
Many a neat perplexity,
Many a turn and many a cross-
Track they redeem a bank of moss,
Spongy and swelling, and far more

Mickle, much.
Carries hay in's horn (fœnum habet in cornu), is dangerous.
Peltish, angry.
Redeem, gain.

Soft than the finest Lemster ore,
Mildly disparkling like those fires
Which break from the enjewell'd tyres
Of curious brides ; or like those mites
Of candi'd dew in moony nights.
Upon this convex all the flowers
Nature begets by th' sun and showers,
Are to a wild digestion brought,
As if love's sampler here was wrought :
Or Citherea's ceston, which
All with temptation doth bewitch.
Sweet airs move here, and more divine
Made by the breath of great-eyed kine,
Who, as they low, impearl with milk
The four-leaved grass or moss like silk.
The breath of monkeys met to mix
With musk-flies are th' aromatics
Which 'cense this arch ; and here and there
And farther off, and everywhere
Throughout that brave mosaic yard,
Those picks or diamonds in the card
With peeps of hearts, of club, and spade
Are here most neatly inter-laid
Many a counter, many a die,
Half-rotten and without an eye
Lies hereabouts ; and, for to pave

Lemster ore, Leominster wool.

Tyres, head-dresses.

Picks, diamonds on playing-cards were so called from
their points.

Peeps, pips.

HESPERIDES.

The excellency of this cave,
Squirrels' and children's teeth late shed
Are neatly here enchequered
With brownest toadstones, and the gum
That shines upon the bluer plum.
The nails fallen off by whitflaws: art's
Wise hand enchasing here those warts
Which we to others, from ourselves,
Sell, and brought hither by the elves.
The tempting mole, stolen from the neck
Of the shy virgin, seems to deck
The holy entrance, where within
The room is hung with the blue skin
Of shifted snake: enfriez'd throughout
With eyes of peacocks' trains and trout-
Flies' curious wings; and these among
Those silver pence that cut the tongue
Of the red infant, neatly hung.
The glow-worm's eyes; the shining scales
Of silv'ry fish; wheat straws, the snail's ,
Soft candle light; the kitling's eyne;
Corrupted wood; serve here for shine.
No glaring light of bold-fac'd day,
Or other over-radiant ray,
Ransacks this room; but what weak beams
Can make reflected from these gems
And multiply; such is the light,
But ever doubtful day or night.

Whitflaws, whitlows.
Corrupted, *i.e.*, phosphorescent.

By this quaint taper light he winds
His errors up; and now he finds
His moon-tann'd Mab, as somewhat sick,
And (love knows) tender as a chick.
Upon six plump dandillions, high-
Rear'd, lies her elvish majesty :
Whose woolly bubbles seem'd to drown
Her Mabship in obedient down.
For either sheet was spread the caul
That doth the infant's face enthral,
When it is born (by some enstyl'd
The lucky omen of the child),
And next to these two blankets o'er-
Cast of the finest gossamore.
And then a rug of carded wool,
Which, sponge-like drinking in the dull
Light of the moon, seemed to comply,
Cloud-like, the dainty deity.
Thus soft she lies : and overhead
A spinner's circle is bespread
With cob-web curtains, from the roof
So neatly sunk as that no proof
Of any tackling can declare
What gives it hanging in the air.
The fringe about this are those threads
Broke at the loss of maidenheads :

Winds his errors up, brings his wanderings to an end.
Dandillions, dandelions.
Comply, embrace.
Spinner, spider.
Proof, sign.

And, all behung with these, pure pearls,
Dropp'd from the eyes of ravish'd girls
Or writhing brides; when (panting) they
Give unto love the straiter way.
For music now, he has the cries
Of feigned-lost virginities;
The which the elves make to excite
A more unconquered appetite.
The king's undrest; and now upon
The gnat's watchword the elves are gone.
And now the bed, and Mab possess'd
Of this great little kingly guest;
We'll nobly think, what's to be done,
He'll do no doubt; *this flax is spun.*

444. TO HIS PECULIAR FRIEND, MR. THOMAS SHAPCOTT, LAWYER.

I 'VE paid thee what I promis'd; that's not all;
Besides I give thee here a verse that shall
(When hence thy circummortal part is gone),
Arch-like, hold up thy name's inscription.
Brave men can't die, whose candid actions are
Writ in the poet's endless calendar :
Whose vellum and whose volume is the sky,
And the pure stars the praising poetry.

                                        Farewell

  Circummortal, more than morta
  Candid, fair.

445. TO JULIA IN THE TEMPLE.

BESIDES us two, i' th' temple here's not one
To make up now a congregation.
Let's to the altar of perfumes then go,
And say short prayers; and when we have done so,
Then we shall see, how in a little space
Saints will come in to fill each pew and place.

446. TO OENONE.

WHAT conscience, say, is it in thee,
    When I a heart had one,
To take away that heart from me,
    And to retain thy own?

For shame or pity now incline
    To play a loving part;
Either to send me kindly thine,
    Or give me back my heart.

Covet not both; but if thou dost
    Resolve to part with neither,
Why! yet to show that thou art just,
    Take me and mine together.

447. HIS WEAKNESS IN WOES.

I CANNOT suffer; and in this my part
Of patience wants. *Grief breaks the stoutest heart.*

448. FAME MAKES US FORWARD.

To print our poems, the propulsive cause
Is fame—the breath of popular applause.

449. TO GROVES.

YE silent shades, whose each tree here
Some relique of a saint doth wear,
Who, for some sweetheart's sake, did prove
The fire and martyrdom of love :
Here is the legend of those saints
That died for love, and their complaints:
Their wounded hearts and names we find
Encarv'd upon the leaves and rind.
Give way, give way to me, who come
Scorch'd with the self-same martyrdom :
And have deserv'd as much (love knows)
As to be canonis'd 'mongst those
Whose deeds and deaths here written are
Within your greeny calendar :
By all those virgins' fillets hung
Upon your boughs, and requiems sung
For saints and souls departed hence
(Here honour'd still with frankincense);
By all those tears that have been shed,
As a drink-offering to the dead ;
By all those true love-knots that be
With mottoes carv'd on every tree ;
By sweet Saint Phyllis pity me:

Phyllis, the Thracian princess who hanged herself for
love of Demophoon.

By dear Saint Iphis, and the rest
Of all those other saints now blest,
Me, me, forsaken, here admit
Among your myrtles to be writ:
That my poor name may have the glory
To live remembered in your story.

450. AN EPITAPH UPON A VIRGIN.

HERE a solemn fast we keep,
While all beauty lies asleep
Hush'd be all things—no noise here—
But the toning of a tear:
Or a sigh of such as bring
Cowslips for her covering.

451. TO THE RIGHT GRACIOUS PRINCE, LODOWICK, DUKE OF RICHMOND AND LENNOX.

OF all those three brave brothers fall'n i' th' war
(Not without glory), noble sir, you are,
Despite of all concussions, left the stem
To shoot forth generations like to them.
Which may be done, if, sir, you can beget
Men in their substance, not in counterfeit,
Such essences as those three brothers; known
Eternal by their own production.
Of whom, from fame's white trumpet, this I'll tell,

Iphis, a Cyprian youth who hanged himself for love of Anaxaretes.

Worthy their everlasting chronicle :
Never since first Bellona us'd a shield,
Such three brave brothers fell in Mars his field.
These were those three Horatii Rome did boast,
Rome's were these three Horatii we have lost.
One Cœur-de-Lion had that age long since ;
This, three ; which three, you make up four, brave
    prince.

452. TO JEALOUSY.

O JEALOUSY, that art
The canker of the heart ;
    And mak'st all hell
    Where thou do'st dwell ;
    For pity be
No fury, or no firebrand to me.

Far from me I'll remove
All thoughts of irksome love ;
    And turn to snow,
    Or crystal grow,
    To keep still free,
O ! soul-tormenting jealousy, from thee.

453. TO LIVE FREELY.

LET's live in haste ; use pleasures while we may ;
Could life return, 'twould never lose a day.

455. HIS ALMS.

HERE, here I live,
And somewhat give
Of what I have
To those who crave,
Little or much,
My alms is such ;
But if my deal
Of oil and meal
Shall fuller grow,
More I'll bestow ;
Meantime be it
E'en but a bit,
Or else a crumb,
The scrip hath some.

456. UPON HIMSELF.

COME, leave this loathed country life, and then
Grow up to be a Roman citizen.
Those mites of time, which yet remain unspent,
Waste thou in that most civil government.
Get their comportment and the gliding tongue
Of those mild men thou art to live among;
Then, being seated in that smoother sphere,
Decree thy everlasting topic there;
And to the farm-house ne'er return at all :
Though granges do not love thee, cities shall.

Deal, portion.

457. TO ENJOY THE TIME.

WHILE Fates permit us let's be merry,
Pass all we must the fatal ferry;　..
And this our life too whirls away
With the rotation of the day.

458. UPON LOVE.

LOVE, I have broke
　　Thy yoke,
The neck is free;
But when I'm next
　　Love-vexed,
Then shackle me.

'Tis better yet
　　To fret
The feet or hands,
Than to enthral
　　Or gall
The neck with bands.

459. TO THE RIGHT HONOURABLE MILDMAY, EARL OF WESTMORELAND.

YOU are a lord, an earl, nay more, a man,
Who writes sweet numbers well as any can;
If so, why then are not these verses hurled,
Like Sybil's leaves, throughout the ample world?

What is a jewel if it be not set
Forth by a ring or some rich carcanet?
But being so, then the beholders cry:
See, see a gem as rare as Belus' eye.
Then public praise does run upon the stone,
For a most rich, a rare, a precious one.
Expose your jewels then unto the view,
That we may praise them, or themselves prize you.
Virtue concealed, with Horace you'll confess,
Differs not much from drowsy slothfulness.

460. THE PLUNDER.

I AM of all bereft,
Save but some few beans left,
Whereof, at last, to make
For me and mine a cake,
Which eaten, they and I
Will say our grace, and die.

461. LITTLENESS NO CAUSE OF LEANNESS.

ONE feeds on lard, and yet is lean,
And I but feasting with a bean
Grow fat and smooth.   The reason is:
Jove prospers my meat more than his.

Belus' eye, the eye onyx.   "The stone called Belus'
eie is white, and hath within it a black apple." (Hol-
land's *Pliny.*)

464. THE JIMMALL RING OR TRUE-LOVE KNOT.

THOU sent'st to me a true love-knot, but I
Returned a ring of jimmals to imply
Thy love had one knot, mine a triple tie.

465. THE PARTING VERSE OR CHARGE TO HIS
SUPPOSED WIFE WHEN HE TRAVELLED.

Go hence, and with this parting kiss,
Which joins two souls, remember this:
Though thou be'st young, kind, soft, and fair
And may'st draw thousands with a hair;
Yet let these glib temptations be
Furies to others, friends to me.
Look upon all, and though on fire
Thou set their hearts, let chaste desire
Steer thee to me, and think, me gone,
In having all, that thou hast none.
Nor so immured would I have
Thee live, as dead and in thy grave;
But walk abroad, yet wisely well
Stand for my coming, sentinel.
And think, as thou do'st walk the street,
Me or my shadow thou do'st meet.
I know a thousand greedy eyes
Will on thy feature tyrannise
In my short absence, yet behold
Them like some picture, or some mould

Jimmal or *gimmal*, double or triple ring.

Fashion'd like thee, which, though 't have ears
And eyes, it neither sees or hears.
Gifts will be sent, and letters, which
Are the expressions of that itch,
And salt, which frets thy suitors; fly
Both, lest thou lose thy liberty;
For, that once lost, thou't fall to one,
Then prostrate to a million.
But if they woo thee, do thou say,
As that chaste Queen of Ithaca
Did to her suitors, this web done,
(Undone as oft as done), I'm won;
I will not urge thee, for I know,
Though thou art young, thou canst say no,
And no again, and so deny
Those thy lust-burning incubi.
Let them enstyle thee fairest fair,
The pearl of princes, yet despair
That so thou art, because thou must
Believe love speaks it not, but lust;
And this their flattery does commend
Thee chiefly for their pleasure's end.
I am not jealous of thy faith,
Or will be, for the axiom saith:
He that doth suspect does haste
A gentle mind to be unchaste.
No, live thee to thy self, and keep
Thy thoughts as cold as is thy sleep,

Queen of Ithaca, Penelope.
Incubi, adulterous spirits.

And let thy dreams be only fed
With this, that I am in thy bed;
And thou, then turning in that sphere,
Waking shalt find me sleeping there.
But yet if boundless lust must scale
Thy fortress, and will needs prevail,
And wildly force a passage in,
Banish consent, and 'tis no sin
Of thine; so Lucrece fell and the
Chaste Syracusian Cyane.
So Medullina fell; yet none
Of these had imputation
For the least trespass, 'cause the mind
Here was not with the act combin'd.
The body sins not, 'tis the will
That makes the action, good or ill.
And if thy fall should this way come,
Triumph in such a martyrdom.
I will not over-long enlarge
To thee this my religious charge.
Take this compression, so by this
Means I shall know what other kiss
Is mixed with mine, and truly know,
Returning, if't be mine or no:
Keep it till then; and now, my spouse,
For my wished safety pay thy vows

Cyane, a nymph of Syracuse, ravished by her father
whom (and herself) she slew.
Medullina, a Roman virgin who endured a like fate.
Compression, embrace.

And prayers to Venus ; if it please
The great blue ruler of the seas,
Not many full-faced moons shall wane,
Lean-horn'd, before I come again
As one triumphant, when I fir.d
In thee all faith of womankind.
Nor would I have thee think that thou
Had'st power thyself to keep this vow,
But, having 'scaped temptation's shelf,
Know virtue taught thee, not thyself.

466. TO HIS KINSMAN, SIR THOS. SOAME.

SEEING thee, Soame, I see a goodly man,
And in that good a great patrician.
Next to which two, among the city powers
And thrones, thyself one of those senators ;
Not wearing purple only for the show,
As many conscripts of the city do,
But for true service, worthy of that gown,
The golden chain, too, and the civic crown.

467. TO BLOSSOMS.

FAIR pledges of a fruitful tree,
     Why do ye fall so fast ?
     Your date is not so past
But you may stay yet here a while,
     To blush and gently smile ;
     And go at last.

Conscripts, " patres conscripti," aldermen.

What! were ye born to be
  An hour or half's delight,
  And so to bid good-night?
'Twas pity Nature brought ye forth
  Merely to show your worth,
    And lose you quite.

But you are lovely leaves, where we
  May read how soon things have
  Their end, though ne'er so brave:
And after they have shown their pride
  Like you a while, they glide
    Into the grave.

468. MAN'S DYING-PLACE UNCERTAIN.

MAN knows where first he ships himself, but he
Never can tell where shall his landing be.

469. NOTHING FREE-COST.

NOTHING comes free-cost here; Jove will not let
His gifts go from him, if not bought with sweat.

472. FEW FORTUNATE.

MANY we are, and yet but few possess
Those fields of everlasting happiness.

471. TO PERENNA.

How long, Perenna, wilt thou see
Me languish for the love of thee?
Consent, and play a friendly part
To save, when thou may'st kill a heart.

472. TO THE LADIES.

TRUST me, ladies, I will do
Nothing to distemper you;
If I any fret or vex,
Men they shall be, not your sex.

473. THE OLD WIVES' PRAYER.

HOLY rood, come forth and shield
Us i' th' city and the field:
Safely guard us, now and aye,
From the blast that burns by day;
And those sounds that us affright
In the dead of dampish night.
Drive all hurtful fiends us fro,
By the time the cocks first crow.

475. UPON HIS DEPARTURE HENCE.

THUS I
Pass by,
And die:
As one
Unknown

And gone:
I'm made
A shade,
And laid
I' th' grave :
There have
My cave,
Where tell
I dwell.
Farewell.

478. THE WASSAIL.

GIVE way, give way, ye gates, and win
An easy blessing to your bin
And basket, by our entering in.

May both with manchet stand replete;
Your larders, too, so hung with meat,
That though a thousand, thousand eat,

Yet, ere twelve moons shall whirl about
Their silv'ry spheres, there's none may doubt
But more's sent in than was served out.

Next, may your dairies prosper so
As that your pans no ebb may know;
But if they do, the more to flow,

Like to a solemn sober stream
Bank'd all with lilies, and the cream
Of sweetest cowslips filling them.

Manchet, fine white bread.

Then, may your plants be prest with fruit,
Nor bee, or hive you have be mute;
But sweetly sounding like a lute.

Next, may your duck and teeming hen
Both to the cock's tread say Amen;
And for their two eggs render ten.

Last, may your harrows, shears, and ploughs,
Your stacks, your stocks, your sweetest mows,
All prosper by our virgin vows.

Alas! we bless, but see none here
That brings us either ale or beer;
In a dry house all things are near.

Let's leave a longer time to wait,
Where rust and cobwebs bind the gate,
And all live here with needy fate.

Where chimneys do for ever weep
For want of warmth, and stomachs keep,
With noise, the servants' eyes from sleep.

It is in vain to sing, or stay
Our free feet here; but we'll away:
Yet to the Lares this we'll say:

The time will come when you'll be sad
And reckon this for fortune bad,
T'ave lost the good ye might have had.

> *Prest*, laden.
> *Near*, penurious.
> *Leave to wait*, cease waiting.

477. UPON A LADY FAIR BUT FRUITLESS.

TWICE has Pudica been a bride, and led
By holy Hymen to the nuptial bed.
Two youths she's known thrice two, and twice three
    years;
Yet not a lily from the bed appears:
Nor will; for why, Pudica this may know,
Trees never bear unless they first do blow.

478. HOW SPRINGS CAME FIRST.

THESE springs were maidens once that lov'd,
But lost to that they most approv'd:
My story tells by Love they were
Turn'd to these springs which we see here;
The pretty whimpering that they make,
When of the banks their leave they take,
Tells ye but this, they are the same,
In nothing chang'd but in their name.

479. TO ROSEMARY AND BAYS.

MY wooing's ended: now my wedding's near
When gloves are giving, gilded be you there.

481. UPON A SCAR IN A VIRGIN'S FACE.

'TIS heresy in others: in your face
That scar's no schism, but the sign of grace.

15

482. UPON HIS EYESIGHT FAILING HIM.

I BEGIN to wane in sight;
Shortly I shall bid good-night:
Then no gazing more about,
When the tapers once are out.

483. TO HIS WORTHY FRIEND, M. THOS. FALCONBIRGE.

STAND with thy graces forth, brave man, and rise
High with thine own auspicious destinies:
Nor leave the search, and proof, till thou canst find
These, or those ends, to which thou wast design'd.
Thy lucky genius and thy guiding star
Have made thee prosperous in thy ways thus far:
Nor will they leave thee till they both have shown
Thee to the world a prime and public one.
Then, when thou see'st thine age all turn'd to gold,
Remember what thy Herrick thee foretold,
When at the holy threshold of thine house
He boded good luck to thy self and spouse.
Lastly, be mindful, when thou art grown great,
*That towers high rear'd dread most the lightning's
     threat:*
Whenas the humble cottages not fear
The cleaving bolt of Jove the thunderer.

484. UPON JULIA'S HAIR FILL'D WITH DEW.

DEW sat on Julia's hair
    And spangled too,
Like leaves that laden are
    With trembling dew:

Or glitter'd to my sight,
    As when the beams
Have their reflected light
    Danc'd by the streams.

485. ANOTHER ON HER.

How can I choose but love and follow her
Whose shadow smells like milder pomander?
How can I choose but kiss her, whence does come
The storax, spikenard, myrrh, and laudanum?

486. LOSS FROM THE LEAST.

GREAT men by small means oft are overthrown;
He's lord of thy life who contemns his own.

487. REWARD AND PUNISHMENTS.

ALL things are open to these two events,
Or to rewards, or else to punishments.

488. SHAME NO STATIST.

SHAME is a bad attendant to a state:
He rents his crown that fears the people's hate.

Pomander, ball of scent.

489. TO SIR CLIPSEBY CREW.

SINCE to the country first I came
I have lost my former flame :
And, methinks, I not inherit,
As I did, my ravish'd spirit.
If I write a verse or two,
'Tis with very much ado ;
In regard I want that wine
Which should conjure up a line.
Yet, though now of Muse bereft,
I have still the manners left
For to thank you, noble sir,
For those gifts you do confer
Upon him who only can
Be in prose a grateful man.

490. UPON HIMSELF.

I COULD never love indeed ;
Never see mine own heart bleed :
Never crucify my life,
Or for widow, maid, or wife.

I could never seek to please
One or many mistresses :
Never like their lips to swear
Oil of roses still smelt there.

I could never break my sleep,
Fold mine arms, sob, sigh, or weep :

Never beg, or humbly woo
With oaths and lies, as others do.

I could never walk alone;
Put a shirt of sackcloth on:
Never keep a fast, or pray
For good luck in love that day.

But have hitherto liv'd free
As the air that circles me:
And kept credit with my heart,
Neither broke i' th' whole, or part.

491. FRESH CHEESE AND CREAM.

WOULD ye have fresh cheese and cream?
Julia's breast can give you them:
And, if more, each nipple cries:
To your cream here's strawberries.

492. AN ECLOGUE OR PASTORAL BETWEEN ENDYMION
PORTER AND LYCIDAS HERRICK,
SET AND SUNG.

End. AH! Lycidas, come tell me why
Thy whilom merry oat
By thee doth so neglected lie,
And never purls a note?

I prithee speak. *Lyc.* I will. *End.* Say on.
Lyc. 'Tis thou, and only thou,
That art the cause, Endymion. .
End. For love's sake, tell me how.

Oat, oaten pipe.

Lyc. In this regard: that thou do'st play
  Upon another plain,
 And for a rural roundelay
  Strik'st now a courtly strain.

 Thou leav'st our hills, our dales, our bowers,
  Our finer fleeced sheep,
 Unkind to us, to spend thine hours
  Where shepherds should not keep.

 I mean the court: Let Latmos be
  My lov'd Endymion's court.
End. But I the courtly state would see.
Lyc. Then see it in report.

 What has the court to do with swains,
  Where Phyllis is not known?
 Nor does it mind the rustic strains
  Of us, or Corydon.

 Break, if thou lov'st us, this delay.
End. Dear Lycidas, e're long
 I vow, by Pan, to come away
  And pipe unto thy song.

 Then Jessamine, with Florabell,
  And dainty Amaryllis,
 With handsome-handed Drosomell
  Shall prank thy hook with lilies.

Prank, bedeck.   *Drosomell*, honey dew.

Lyc. Then Tityrus, and Corydon,
    And Thyrsis, they shall follow
With all the rest; while thou alone
    Shalt lead like young Apollo.

And till thou com'st, thy Lycidas,
    In every genial cup,
Shall write in spice: Endymion 'twas
    That kept his piping up.

And, my most lucky swain, when I shall live to see
Endymion's moon to fill up full, remember me:
Meantime, let Lycidas have leave to pipe to thee.

493. TO A BED OF TULIPS.

BRIGHT tulips, we do know
    You had your coming hither,
And fading-time does show
    That ye must quickly wither.

Your sisterhoods may stay,
    And smile here for your hour;
But die ye must away,
    Even as the meanest flower.

Come, virgins, then, and see
    Your frailties, and bemoan ye;
For, lost like these, 'twill be
    As time had never known ye.

494. A CAUTION.

THAT love last long, let it thy first care be
To find a wife that is most fit for thee.
Be she too wealthy or too poor, be sure
Love in extremes can never long endure.

495. TO THE WATER NYMPHS DRINKING AT THE FOUNTAIN.

REACH, with your whiter hands, to me
   Some crystal of the spring ;
And I about the cup shall see
   Fresh lilies flourishing.

Or else, sweet nymphs, do you but this,
   To th' glass your lips incline ;
And I shall see by that one kiss
   The water turn'd to wine.

496. TO HIS HONOURED KINSMAN, SIR RICHARD STONE.

To this white temple of my heroes here,
Beset with stately figures everywhere
Of such rare saintships, who did here consume
Their lives in sweets, and left in death perfume,
Come, thou brave man ! And bring with thee a
   stone
Unto thine own edification.
High are these statues here, besides no less
Strong than the heavens for everlastingness :
Where build aloft ; and, being fix'd by these,
Set up thine own eternal images.

497. UPON A FLY.

A GOLDEN fly one show'd to me,
Clos'd in a box of ivory,
Where both seem'd proud: the fly to have
His burial in an ivory grave;
The ivory took state to hold
A corpse as bright as burnish'd gold.
One fate had both, both equal grace;
The buried, and the burying-place.
Not Virgil's gnat, to whom the spring
All flowers sent to's burying;
Not Martial's bee, which in a bead
Of amber quick was buried;
Nor that fine worm that does inter
Herself i' th' silken sepulchre;
Nor my rare Phil,* that lately was
With lilies tomb'd up in a glass;
More honour had than this same fly,
Dead, and closed up in ivory.

499. TO JULIA.

JULIA, when thy Herrick dies,
Close thou up thy poet's eyes:
And his last breath, let it be
Taken in by none but thee.

Virgil's gnat, see 256.   *Martial's bee*, see Note.
    **Sparrow.* (Note in the original edition.)

500. TO MISTRESS DOROTHY PARSONS.

IF thou ask me, dear, wherefore
I do write of thee no more,
I must answer, sweet, thy part
Less is here than in my heart.

502. HOW HE WOULD DRINK HIS WINE.

FILL me my wine in crystal; thus, and thus
I see't in's *puris naturalibus :*
Unmix'd.   I love to have it smirk and shine;
'Tis sin I know, 'tis sin to throttle wine.
What madman's he, that when it sparkles so,
Will cool his flames or quench his fires with snow?

503. HOW MARIGOLDS CAME YELLOW.

JEALOUS girls these sometimes were,
While they liv'd or lasted here :
Turn'd to flowers, still they be
Yellow, mark'd for jealousy.

504. THE BROKEN CRYSTAL.

To fetch me wine my Lucia went,
Bearing a crystal continent :
But, making haste, it came to pass
She brake in two the purer glass,
Then smil'd, and sweetly chid her speed ;
So with a blush beshrew'd the deed.

Continent, holder.

505. PRECEPTS.

GOOD precepts we must firmly hold,
By daily learning we wax old.

506. TO THE RIGHT HONOURABLE EDWARD, EARL OF DORSET.

IF I dare write to you, my lord, who are
Of your own self a public theatre,
And, sitting, see the wiles, ways, walks of wit,
And give a righteous judgment upon it,
What need I care, though some dislike me should,
If Dorset say what Herrick writes is good ?
We know y'are learn'd i' th' Muses, and no less
In our state-sanctions, deep or bottomless.
Whose smile can make a poet, and your glance
Dash all bad poems out of countenance ;
So that an author needs no other bays
For coronation than your only praise,
And no one mischief greater than your frown
To null his numbers, and to blast his crown.
Few live the life immortal.   He ensures
His fame's long life who strives to set up yours.

507. UPON HIMSELF.

THOU'RT hence removing (like a shepherd's tent),
And walk thou must the way that others went :
Fall thou must first, then rise to life with these,
Mark'd in thy book for faithful witnesses.

508. HOPE WELL AND HAVE WELL: OR, FAIR
AFTER FOUL WEATHER.

WHAT though the heaven be lowering now,
And look with a contracted brow ?
We shall discover, by-and-by,
A repurgation of the sky ;
And when those clouds away are driven,
Then will appear a cheerful heaven.

509. UPON LOVE.

I HELD Love's head while it did ache;
    But so it chanc'd to be,
The cruel pain did his forsake,
    And forthwith came to me.

Ay me ! how shall my grief be still'd ?
    Or where else shall we find
One like to me, who must be kill'd
    For being too-too kind ?

510. TO HIS KINSWOMAN, MRS. PENELOPE
WHEELER.

NEXT is your lot, fair, to be number'd one,
Here, in my book's canonisation :
Late you come in ; but you a saint shall be,
In chief, in this poetic liturgy.

511. ANOTHER UPON HER.

FIRST, for your shape, the curious cannot show
Any one part that's dissonant in you:
And 'gainst your chaste behaviour there's no plea,
Since you are known to be Penelope.
Thus fair and clean you are, although there be
A mighty strife 'twixt form and chastity.

513. CROSS AND PILE.

FAIR and foul days trip cross and pile; the fair
Far less in number than our foul days are.

514. TO THE LADY CREW, UPON THE DEATH OF HER CHILD.

WHY, madam, will ye longer weep,
Whenas your baby's lull'd asleep ?
And (pretty child) feels now no more
Those pains it lately felt before.
All now is silent; groans are fled :
Your child lies still, yet is not dead ;
But rather like a flower hid here
To spring again another year.

Form, beauty.
Trip cross and pile, come haphazard, like the heads
and tails of coins.

515. HIS WINDING-SHEET.

COME thou, who art the wine and wit
  Of all I've writ:
The grace, the glory, and the best
  Piece of the rest.
Thou art of what I did intend
  The all and end;
And what was made, was made to meet
  Thee, thee, my sheet.
Come then, and be to my chaste side
  Both bed and bride.
We two, as reliques left, will have
  One rest, one grave.
And, hugging close, we will not fear
  Lust entering here,
Where all desires are dead or cold
  As is the mould;
And all affections are forgot,
  Or trouble not.
Here, here the slaves and pris'ners be
  From shackles free:
And weeping widows long oppress'd
  Do here find rest.
The wronged client ends his laws
  Here, and his cause.
Here those long suits of chancery lie
  Quiet, or die:
And all Star-Chamber bills do cease,
  Or hold their peace.
Here needs no Court for our Request,
  Where all are best,

All wise, all equal, and all just
  Alike i' th' dust.
Nor need we here to fear the frown
  Of court or crown:
Where fortune bears no sway o'er things,
  There all are kings.
In this securer place we'll keep,
  As lull'd asleep ;
Or for a little time we'll lie
  As robes laid by ;
To be another day re-worn,
  Turn'd, but not torn :
Or, like old testaments engrost,
  Lock'd up, not lost .
And for a while lie here conceal'd,
  To be reveal'd
Next at that great Platonick year,
  And then meet here.

516. TO MISTRESS MARY WILLAND.

ONE more by thee, love, and desert have sent,
T' enspangle this expansive firmament.
O flame of beauty! come, appear, appear
A virgin taper, ever shining here.

Platonick year, the 36,000th year, in which all persons
and things return to their original state.

517. CHANGE GIVES CONTENT.

WHAT now we like anon we disapprove:
The new successor drives away old love.

519. ON HIMSELF.

BORN I was to meet with age,
And to walk life's pilgrimage.
Much I know of time is spent,
Tell I can't what's resident.
Howsoever, cares, adieu!
I'll have nought to say to you:
But I'll spend my coming hours
Drinking wine and crown'd with flowers.

520. FORTUNE FAVOURS.

FORTUNE did never favour one
Fully, without exception;
Though free she be, there's something yet
Still wanting to her favourite.

521. TO PHYLLIS, TO LOVE AND LIVE WITH HIM.

LIVE, live with me, and thou shalt see
The pleasures I'll prepare for thee;

Resident, remaining.

What sweets the country can afford
Shall bless thy bed and bless thy board.
The soft, sweet moss shall be thy bed
With crawling woodbine over-spread ;
By which the silver-shedding streams
Shall gently melt thee into dreams.
Thy clothing, next, shall be a gown
Made of the fleece's purest down.
The tongues of kids shall be thy meat,
Their milk thy drink ; and thou shalt eat
The paste of filberts for thy bread,
With cream of cowslips buttered ;
Thy feasting-tables shall be hills
With daisies spread and daffodils,
Where thou shalt sit, and red-breast by,
For meat, shall give thee melody.
I'll give thee chains and carcanets
Of primroses and violets.
A bag and bottle thou shalt have,
That richly wrought, and this as brave ;
So that as either shall express
The wearer's no mean shepherdess.
At shearing-times, and yearly wakes,
When Themilis his pastime makes,
There thou shalt be ; and be the wit,
Nay, more, the feast, and grace of it.

Carcanets, necklaces.
Wakes. village feasts on the dedication day of the
church.

On holidays, when virgins meet
To dance the heyes with nimble feet,
Thou shalt come forth, and then appear
The queen of roses for that year;
And having danced, 'bove all the best,
Carry the garland from the rest.
In wicker baskets maids shall bring
To thee, my dearest shepherling,
The blushing apple, bashful pear,
And shame-fac'd plum, all simp'ring there.
Walk in the groves, and thou shalt find
The name of Phyllis in the rind
Of every straight and smooth-skin tree;
Where kissing that, I'll twice kiss thee.
To thee a sheep-hook I will send,
Be-prank'd with ribands to this end;
This, this alluring hook might be
Less for to catch a sheep than me.
Thou shalt have possets, wassails fine,
Not made of ale, but spiced wine,
To make thy maids and self free mirth,
All sitting near the glitt'ring hearth.
Thou shalt have ribands, roses, rings,
Gloves, garters, stockings, shoes, and strings
Of winning colours, that shall move
Others to lust, but me to love.
These, nay, and more, thine own shall be
If thou wilt love, and live with me.

The heyes, a winding, country dance.

Be-prank'd, be-decked.

522. TO HIS KINSWOMAN, MISTRESS SUSANNA HERRICK.

WHEN I consider, dearest, thou dost stay
But here a-while, to languish and decay,
Like to these garden-glories, which here be
The flowery-sweet resemblances of thee ;
With grief of heart, methinks, I thus do cry :
Would thou hadst ne'er been born, or might'st not
    die.

523. UPON MISTRESS SUSANNA SOUTHWELL, HER CHEEKS.

RARE are thy cheeks, Susanna, which do show
Ripe cherries smiling, while that others blow.

524. UPON HER EYES.

CLEAR are her eyes,
  Like purest skies,
Discovering from thence
   A baby there
   That turns each sphere,
Like an Intelligence.

525. UPON HER FEET.

HER pretty feet
Like snails did creep
  A little out, and then,
As if they played at Bo-Peep,
  Did soon draw in again.

A baby, see Note to 38, "To his mistress objecting to him neither toying nor talking".

526. TO HIS HONOURED FRIEND, SIR JOHN MINCE.

FOR civil, clean, and circumcised wit,
And for the comely carriage of it,
Thou art the man, the only man best known,
Mark'd for the true wit of a million :
From whom we'll reckon. Wit came in but since
The calculation of thy birth, brave Mince.

527. UPON HIS GREY HAIRS.

FLY me not, though I be grey :
Lady, this I know you'll say ;
Better look the roses red
When with white commingled.
Black your hairs are, mine are white ;
This begets the more delight,
When things meet most opposite :
As in pictures we descry
Venus standing Vulcan by.

528. ACCUSATION.

IF accusation only can draw blood,
None shall be guiltless, be he ne'er so good.

529. PRIDE ALLOWABLE IN POETS.

As thou deserv'st, be proud ; then gladly let
The Muse give thee the Delphic coronet.

530. A VOW TO MINERVA.

GODDESS, I begin an art ;
Come thou in, with thy best part
For to make the texture lie
Each way smooth and civilly ;
And a broad-fac'd owl shall be
Offer'd up with vows to thee.

534. TO ELECTRA.

'TIS evening, my sweet,
And dark, let us meet ;
Long time w'ave here been a-toying,
And never, as yet,
That season could get
Wherein t'ave had an enjoying.

For pity or shame,
Then let not love's flame
Be ever and ever a-spending ;
Since now to the port
The path is but short,
And yet our way has no ending.

Time flies away fast,
Our hours do waste,
The while we never remember
How soon our life, here,
Grows old with the year
That dies with the next December.

Civilly, orderly.
Owl, the bird sacred to Athene or Minerva.

535. DISCORD NOT DISADVANTAGEOUS.

FORTUNE no higher project can devise
Than to sow discord 'mongst the enemies.

536. ILL GOVERNMENT.

PREPOSTEROUS is that government, and rude,
When kings obey the wilder multitude.

537. TO MARIGOLDS.

GIVE way, and be ye ravish'd by the sun,
And hang the head whenas the act is done,
Spread as he spreads, wax less as he does wane ;
And as he shuts, close up to maids again.

538. TO DIANEME.

GIVE me one kiss
    And no more :
If so be this
    Makes you poor,
To enrich you,
    I'll restore
For that one two
    Thousand score.

Preposterous, lit. hind-part before.

539. TO JULIA, THE FLAMINICA DIALIS OR QUEEN-PRIEST.

THOU know'st, my Julia, that it is thy turn
This morning's incense to prepare and burn.
The chaplet and Inarculum * here be,
With the white vestures, all attending thee.
This day the queen-priest thou art made, t' appease
Love for our very many trespasses.
One chief transgression is, among the rest,
Because with flowers her temple was not dressed ;
The next, because her altars did not shine
With daily fires ; the last, neglect of wine ;
For which her wrath is gone forth to consume
Us all, unless preserv'd by thy perfume.
Take then thy censer, put in fire, and thus,
O pious priestess! make a peace for us.
For our neglect Love did our death decree ;
That we escape *Redemption comes by thee.*

540. ANACREONTIC.

BORN I was to be old,
　　And for to die here :
After that, in the mould
　　Long for to lie here.
But before that day comes
　　Still I be bousing,
For I know in the tombs
　　There's no carousing.

* A twig of a pomegranate, which the queen-priest
did use to wear on her head at sacrificing. (Note in the
original edition.)

541. MEAT WITHOUT MIRTH.

EATEN I have; and though I had good cheer,
I did not sup, because no friends were there.
Where mirth and friends are absent when we dine
Or sup, there wants the incense and the wine.

542. LARGE BOUNDS DO BUT BURY US.

ALL things o'er-ruled are here by chance:
The greatest man's inheritance,
Where'er the lucky lot doth fall,
Serves but for place of burial.

543. UPON URSLEY.

URSLEY, she thinks those velvet patches grace
The candid temples of her comely face;
But he will say, whoe'er those circlets seeth,
They be but signs of Ursley's hollow teeth.

544. AN ODE TO SIR CLIPSEBY CREW.

HERE we securely live and eat
The cream of meat,
And keep eternal fires,
By which we sit, and do divine
As wine
And rage inspires.

Securely, free from care.

If full we charm, then call upon
    Anacreon
  To grace the frantic thyrse;
And having drunk, we raise a shout
    Throughout
  To praise his verse.

Then cause we Horace to be read,
    Which sung, or said,
  A goblet to the brim
Of lvric wine, both swell'd and crown'd,
    Around
  We quaff to him.

Thus, thus we live, and spend the hours
    In wine and flowers,
  And make the frolic year,
The month, the week, the instant day
    To stay
  The longer here.

Come then, brave knight, and see the cell
    Wherein I dwell,
  And my enchantments too,
Which love and noble freedom is;
    And this
  Shall fetter you.

      Thyrse, a Bacchic staff.
      Instant, oncoming.

Take horse, and come, or be so kind
To send your mind,
Though but in numbers few,
And I shall think I have the heart,
Or part
Of Clipseby Crew.

545. TO HIS WORTHY KINSMAN, MR. STEPHEN SOAME.

NOR is my number full till I inscribe
Thee, sprightly Soame, one of my righteous tribe;
A tribe of one lip, leaven, and of one
Civil behaviour, and religion;
A stock of saints, where ev'ry one doth wear
A stole of white, and canonised here;
Among which holies be thou ever known,
Brave kinsman, mark'd out with the whiter stone
Which seals thy glory, since I do prefer
Thee here in my eternal calender.

546. TO HIS TOMB-MAKER.

Go I must; when I am gone,
Write but this upon my stone:
Chaste I lived, without a wife,
That's the story of my life.
Strewings need none, every flower
Is in this word, bachelour.

Numbers, verses.

547. GREAT SPIRITS SUPERVIVE.

OUR mortal parts may wrapp'd in sear-cloths lie:
Great spirits never with their bodies die.

548. NONE FREE FROM FAULT.

OUT of the world he must, who once comes in.
No man exempted is from death, or sin.

549. UPON HIMSELF BEING BURIED.

LET me sleep this night away,
Till the dawning of the day;
Then at th' opening of mine eyes
I, and all the world, shall rise.

550. PITY TO THE PROSTRATE.

'TIS worse than barbarous cruelty to show
No part of pity on a conquered foe.

552. HIS CONTENT IN THE COUNTRY.

HERE, here I live with what my board
Can with the smallest cost afford.
Though ne'er so mean the viands be,
They well content my Prew and me.
Or pea, or bean, or wort, or beet,
Whatever comes, content makes sweet.

Prew, i.e., his servant, Prudence Baldwin.

Here we rejoice, because no rent
We pay for our poor tenement,
Wherein we rest, and never fear
The landlord or the usurer.
The quarter-day does ne'er affright
Our peaceful slumbers in the night.
We eat our own and batten more,
Because we feed on no man's score ;
But pity those whose flanks grow great,
Swell'd with the lard of others' meat.
We bless our fortunes when we see
Our own beloved privacy ;
And like our living, where we're known
To very few, or else to none.

553. THE CREDIT OF THE CONQUEROR.

HE who commends the vanquished, speaks the power
And glorifies the worthy conqueror.

554. ON HIMSELF.

SOME parts may perish, die thou canst not all :
The most of thee shall 'scape the funeral.

556. THE FAIRIES.

IF ye will with Mab find grace,
Set each platter in his place ;
Rake the fire up, and get
Water in, ere sun be set.
Wash your pails, and cleanse your dairies ;
Sluts are loathsome to the fairies ;
Sweep your house, who doth not so,
Mab will pinch her by the toe.

557. TO HIS HONOURED FRIEND, M. JOHN WEARE, COUNCILLOR.

DID I or love, or could I others draw
To the indulgence of the rugged law,
The first foundation of that zeal should be
By reading all her paragraphs in thee,
Who dost so fitly with the laws unite,
As if you two were one hermaphrodite.
Nor courts[t] thou her because she's well attended
With wealth, but for those ends she was intended:
Which were,—and still her offices are known,—
Law is to give to ev'ry one his own;
To shore the feeble up against the strong,
To shield the stranger and the poor from wrong.
This was the founder's grave and good intent:
To keep the outcast in his tenement,
To free the orphan from that wolf-like man,
Who is his butcher more than guardian;
To dry the widow's tears, and stop her swoons,
By pouring balm and oil into her wounds.
This was the old way; and 'tis yet thy course
To keep those pious principles in force.
Modest I will be; but one word I'll say,
Like to a sound that's vanishing away,
Sooner the inside of thy hand shall grow
Hisped and hairy, ere thy palm shall know
A postern-bribe took, or a forked fee,

> *Hisped* (*hispidus*), rough with hairs.
> *Postern-bribe*, a back-door bribe.
> *Forked fee*, a fee from both sides in a case; cp. Ben
> Jonson's *Volpone:* "Give forked counsel, take provoking
> gold on either hand".

To fetter Justice, when she might be free.
Eggs I'll not shave ; but yet, brave man, if I
Was destin'd forth to golden sovereignty,
A prince I'd be, that I might thee prefer
To be my counsel both and chancellor.

560. THE WATCH.

MAN is a watch, wound up at first, but never
Wound up again: once down, he's down for ever.
The watch once down, all motions then do cease ;
And man's pulse stop'd, all passions sleep in peace.

561. LINES HAVE THEIR LININGS, AND BOOKS
THEIR BUCKRAM.

As in our clothes, so likewise he who looks,
Shall find much farcing buckram in our books.

562. ART ABOVE NATURE: TO JULIA.

WHEN I behold a forest spread
With silken trees upon thy head,
And when I see that other dress
Of flowers set in comeliness ;
When I behold another grace
In the ascent of curious lace,
Which like a pinnacle doth show
The top, and the top-gallant too.
Then, when I see thy tresses bound
Into an oval, square, or round,

Eggs I'll not shave, a proverb.
Farcing, stuffing.

And knit in knots far more than I
Can tell by tongue, or true-love tie;
Next, when those lawny films I see
Play with a wild civility,
And all those airy silks to flow,
Alluring me, and tempting so:
I must confess mine eye and heart
Dotes less on Nature than on Art.

564. UPON HIS KINSWOMAN, MISTRESS BRIDGET
HERRICK.

SWEET Bridget blush'd, and therewithal
Fresh blossoms from her cheeks did fall.
I thought at first 'twas but a dream,
Till after I had handled them
And smelt them, then they smelt to me
As blossoms of the almond tree.

565. UPON LOVE.

I PLAYED with Love, as with the fire
    The wanton Satyr did;
Nor did I know, or could descry
    What under there was hid.

That Satyr he but burnt his lips;
    But mine's the greater smart,
For kissing Love's dissembling chips
    The fire scorch'd my heart.

Civility, order.
The wanton Satyr, see Note.

566. UPON A COMELY AND CURIOUS MAID.

IF men can say that beauty dies,
Marbles will swear that here it lies.
If, reader, then thou canst forbear
In public loss to shed a tear,
The dew of grief upon this stone
Will tell thee pity thou hast none.

567. UPON THE LOSS OF HIS FINGER.

ONE of the five straight branches of my hand
Is lop'd already, and the rest but stand
Expecting when to fall, which soon will be ;
First dies the leaf, the bough next, next the tree.

568. UPON IRENE.

ANGRY if Irene be
But a minute's life with me :
Such a fire I espy
Walking in and out her eye,
As at once I freeze and fry.

569. UPON ELECTRA'S TEARS.

UPON her cheeks she wept, and from those showers
Sprang up a sweet nativity of flowers.

NOTES.

NOTES.

2. *Whither, mad maiden,* etc. From Martial, I. iv. 11, 12 :—

> Aetherias, lascive, cupis volitare per auras :
> I, fuge ; sed poteras tutior esse domi.

But for the Court. Cp. Martial, I. iv. 3, 4.

4. *While Brutus standeth by.* " Brutus and Cato are commonplaces of examples of severe virtue " : Grosart. But Herrick is translating. This is from Martial, XI. xvi. 9, 10 :—

> Erubuit posuitque meum Lucretia librum,
> Sed coram Bruto ; Brute, recede, leget.

8. *When he would have his verses read.* The thought throughout this poem is taken from Martial, X. xix., beginning :—

> Nec doctum satis et parum severum,
> Sed non rusticulum nimis libellum
> Facundo mea Plinio, Thalia,
> I perfer :

where the address to Thalia perhaps explains Herrick's " do not *thou* rehearse ". The important lines are :—

Sed ne tempore non tuo disertam
Pulses ebria januam, videto.

. . . .

Seras tutior ibis ad lucernas.
Hæc hora est tua, cum furit Lyæus,
Cum regnat rosa, cum madent capilli :
Tunc me vel rigidi legant Catones.

When laurel spirts i' th' fire. Burning bay leaves
was a Christmas observance. Herrick sings:—

" Of crackling laurel, which foresounds
A plenteous harvest to your grounds " :

where compare Tibull. II. v. 81-84. It was also
used by maids as a love omen.

Thyrse . . . sacred Orgies. Herrick's glosses
show that the passage he had in mind was Catullus,
lxiv. 256-269:—

Harum pars tecta quatiebant cuspide thyrsos

. . . .

Pars obscura cavis celebrabant orgia cistis,
Orgia, quæ frustra cupiunt audire profani.

10. *No man at one time can be wise and love.*
Amare et sapere vix deo conceditur. (Publius Syrus.)
The quotation is found in both Burton and Montaigne.

12. *Who fears to ask*, etc. From Seneca, *Hippol.*
594-95. Qui timide rogat . . . docet negare.

15. *Goddess Isis . . . with her scent.* Cp. Plutarch, *De Iside et Osiride*, 15.

17. *He acts the crime.* Seneca: Nil interest faveas
sceleri an illud facias.

18. *Two things odious.* From Ecclus. xxv. 2.

31. *A Sister . . . about I'll lead.* "Have we not power to lead about a sister, a wife?" 1 Cor. ix. 5.

35. *Mercy and Truth live with thee.* 2 Sam. xv. 20.

38. *To please those babies in your eyes.* The phrase "babies [*i.e.*, dolls] in the eyes" is probably only a translation of its metaphor, involved in the use of the Latin *pupilla* (a little girl), or "pupil," for the central spot of the eye. The metaphor doubtless arose from the small reflections of the in-looker, which appear in the eyes of the person gazed at; but we meet with it both intensified, as in the phrase "to look babies in the eyes" (= to peer amorously), and with its origin disregarded, as in Herrick, where the "babies" are the pupils, and have an existence independent of any inlooker.

Small griefs find tongue. Seneca, *Hippol.* 608:

Curæ leves loquuntur, ingentes stupent.

Full casks. So G. Herbert, *Jacula Prudentum* (1640) : Empty vessels sound most.

48. *Thus woe succeeds a woe as wave a wave.* Horace, Ep. II. ii. 176: Velut unda supervenit unda. Κύματα κακῶν and κακῶν τρικυμία are common phrases in Greek tragedy.

49. *Cherry-pit.* Printed in the 1654 edition of *Witts Recreations*, where it appears as :—

"*Nicholas* and *Nell* did lately sit
　　Playing for sport at cherry-pit ;
　　They both did throw, and, having thrown,
　　He got the pit and she the stone ".

51. *Ennobled numbers.* This poem is often quoted to prove that Herrick's country incumbency was

good for his verse; but if the reference be only to his sacred poems or *Noble Numbers* these would rather prove the opposite.

52. *O earth, earth, earth, hear thou my voice.* Jerem. xxii. 29 : O earth, earth, earth, hear the word of the Lord.

56. *Love give me more such nights as these.* A reminiscence of Marlowe's version of Ovid, *Amor.* I. v. 26: "Jove send me more such afternoons as this ".

72. *Upon his Sister-in-law, Mistress Elizabeth Herrick,* wife to his brother Thomas (see *infra,* 106).

74. *Love makes me write what shame forbids to speak.* Ovid, *Phædra to Hippol. :* Dicere quæ puduit scribere jussit amor.

Give me a kiss. Herrick is here imitating the well-known lines of Catullus to Lesbia (*Carm.* v.) :—

> Da mi basia mille, deinde centum,
> Dein mille altera, dein secunda centum,
> Deinde usque altera mille, deinde centum,
> Dein, cum millia multa fecerimus,
> Conturbabimus illa, ne sciamus, etc.

77. *To the King, upon his coming with his army into the west.* Essex had marched into the west in June, 1644, relieved Lyme, and captured royal fortresses in Dorset and Devon. Charles followed him into "the drooping west," and, in September, the Parliamentary infantry were forced to surrender, while Essex himself escaped by sea. Herrick's "white omens" were thus fulfilled.

79. *To the King and Queen upon their unhappy*

distances. Henrietta Maria escaped abroad with the crown jewels in 1642, returned the next year and rejoined Charles in the west in 1644, whence she escaped again to France. This poem has been supposed to refer to domestic dissensions ; but the " ball of strife " is surely the Civil War in general, and the reference to the parting of 1644.

81. *The Cheat of Cupid.* Herrick is here translating " Anacreon," 31 [3] :—

Μεσονυκτίοις ποθ' ὥραις
στρέφεθ' ἡνίκ' Ἄρκτος ἤδη
κατὰ χεῖρα τὴν Βοώτου,
μερόπων δὲ φῦλα πάντα
5 κέαται κόπῳ δαμέντα,
τότ' Ἔρως ἐπισταθείς μευ
θυρέων ἔκοπτ' ὀχῆας.
τίς, ἔφην, θύρας ἀράσσει ;
κατά μευ σχίζεις ὀνείρους.
10 ὁ δ' Ἔρως, ἄνοιγε, φησίν·
βρέφος εἰμί, μὴ φόβησαι·
βρέχομαι δὲ κἀσέληνον
κατὰ νύκτα πεπλάνημαι.
ἐλέησα ταῦτ' ἀκούσας,
15 ἀνὰ δ' εὐθὺ λύχνον ἅψας
ἀνέῳξα, καὶ βρέφος μέν

ἐσορῶ φέροντα τόξον
πτέρυγάς τε καὶ φαρέτρην.
παρὰ δ' ἱστίην καθίσα,
20 παλάμαις τε χεῖρας αὐτοῦ
ἀνέθαλπον, ἐκ δὲ χαίτης
ἀπέθλιβον ὑγρὸν ὕδωρ.
ὁ δ', ἐπεὶ κρύος μεθῆκεν,
φέρε, φησί, πειράσωμεν
25 τόδε τόξον, εἴ τι μοι νῦν
βλάβεται βραχεῖσα νευρή.
τανύει δὲ καί με τύπτει
μέσον ἧπαρ, ὥσπερ οἶστρος·
ἀνὰ δ' ἄλλεται καχάζων,
30 ξένε δ', εἶπε, συγχάρηθι·
κέρας ἀβλαβὲς μὲν ἡμῖν,
σὺ δὲ καρδίην πονήσεις.

Some of his phrases, however, prove that he was occasionally more indebted to the Latin version of Stephanus than to the original.

82. *That for seven lusters I did never come.* The fall of Herrick's father from a window, fifteen months after the poet's birth, was imputed at the time to suicide ; and it has been reasonably conjectured that some mystery may have attached to the place of his

burial. If "seven lusters" can be taken literally for thirty-five years, this poem was written in 1627.

83. *Delight in Disorder.* Cp. Ben Jonson's "Still to be neat, still to be drest," in its turn imitated from one of the *Basia* of Johannes Bonefonius.

85. *Upon Love.* Printed in *Witts Recreations*, 1654. The only variant is "To tell me" for "To signifie" in the third line.

86. *To Dean Bourn.* "We found many persons in the village who could repeat some of his lines, and none who were not acquainted with his 'Farewell to Dean Bourn,' which they said he uttered as he crossed the brook upon being ejected by Cromwell from the vicarage, to which he had been presented by Charles the First. But they added, with an air of innocent triumph, 'he did see it again,' as was the fact after the restoration." Barron Field in *Quarterly Review*, August, 1810. Herrick was ejected in 1648.

A rocky generation! a people currish. Cp. Burton, II.iii.2: a rude . . . uncivil, wild, currish generation.

91. *That man loves not who is not zealous too.* Augustine, *Adv. Adimant.* 13: Qui non zelat, non amat.

92. *The Bag of the Bee.* Printed in *Witts Recreations*, 1654, and in Henry Bold's *Wit a-sporting in a Pleasant Grove of new Fancies*, 1657. Set to music by Henry Lawes.

93. *Luxurious love by wealth is nourished.* Ovid, *Remed. Amor.* 746: Divitiis alitur luxuriosus amor.

95. *Homer himself.* Indignor quandoque bonus dormitat Homerus. Horace, *De Art. Poet.* 359.

100. *To bread and water none is poor.* Seneca,
Excerpt. ii. 887 : Panem et aquam Natura desiderat ;
nemo ad haec pauper est.

Nature with little is content. Seneca, *Ep.* xvi. :
Exiguum Natura desiderat. *Ep.* lx. : parvo Natura
dimittitur.

106. *A Country Life : To his brother, M. Tho.
Herrick.* "Thomas, baptized May 12, 1588, was
placed by his uncle and guardian, Sir William Hey-
rick, with Mr. Massam, a merchant in London ; but
in 1610 he appears to have returned into the country
and to have settled in a small farm. It is supposed
that this Thomas was the father of Thomas Hey-
rick, who in 1668 resided at Market Harborough and
issued a trader's token there, and grandfather to the
Thomas who was curate of Harborough and published some sermons and poems." Hill's *Market
Harborough*, p. 122.

A MS. version of this poem is contained in Ashmole 38, from which Dr. Grosart gives a full collation
on pp. cli.-cliii. of his Memorial Introduction. The
MS. appears to follow an unrevised version of the
poem, and contains a few couplets which Herrick
afterwards thought fit to omit. The most important
passage comes after line 92 : " Virtue had, and
mov'd her sphere ".

" Nor know thy happy and unenvied state
   Owes more to virtue than to fate,
   Or fortune too ; for what the first secures,
   That as herself, or heaven, endures.
   The two last fail, and by experience make
   Known, not they give again, they take."

Thrice and above blest. Felices ter et amplius, Hor. I. *Od.* xiii. 7.

My soul's half: Animæ dimidium meæ, Hor. I. *Od.* iii. 8. The poem is full of such reminiscences: "With holy meal and spirting (MS. crackling) salt" is the "Farre pio et saliente mica" of III. *Od.* xxiii. 20; "Untaught to suffer poverty" the "Indocilis pauperiem pati" of I. *Od.* i. 18; "A heart thrice wall'd" comes from I. *Od.* iii. 9: Illi robur et æs triplex, etc. Similar instances might be multiplied. Note, too, the use of "Lar" and "Genius".

Jove for our labour all things sells us. Epicharm. apud Xenoph. *Memor.* II. i. 20, τῶν πόνων Πωλοῦσιν ἡμῖν πάντα τἀγαθ' οἱ θεοί. Quoted by Montaigne, II. xx.

Wisely true to thine own self. Possibly a Shakespearian reminiscence of the "to thine own self be true" in the speech of Polonius to Laertes, *Hamlet*, I. iii. 78.

A wise man every way lies square. Cp. Arist. *Eth.* I. x. 11, ὡς ἀληθῶς ἀγαθὸς καὶ τετράγωνος ἄνευ ψόγου.

For seldom use commends the pleasure. Voluptates commendat rarior usus. Juvenal, *Sat.* xi. ad fin.

Nor fear or wish your dying day. Summum nec metuas diem, nec optes. Mart. X. xlvii. 13.

112. *To the Earl of Westmoreland.* Mildmay Fane succeeded his father, Thomas Fane, the first earl, in March, 1628. At the outbreak of the Civil War he sided with the king, but after a short imprisonment made his submission to the Parliament, and was relieved of the sequestration of his estates.

He subsequently printed privately a volume of poems, called *Otia Sacra*, which has been re-edited by Dr. Grosart.

117. *To the Patron of Poets, M. End. Porter.* Five of Herrick's poems are addressed to Endymion Porter, who seems to have been looked to as a patron by all the singers of his day. According to the inscription on a medal of him executed by Varin in 1635, he was then forty-eight, so that he was born in 1587, coming into the world at Aston-under-Hill in Gloucestershire. He went with Charles on his trip to Spain, and after his accession became groom of his bedchamber, was active in the king's service during the Civil War, and died in 1649. He was a collector of works of art both for himself and for the king, and encouraged Rob. Dover's Cotswold games by presenting him with a suit of the king's clothes. À Wood tells us this, and mentions also that he was a friend of Donne, that Gervase Warmsely dedicated his *Virescit Vulnere Virtus* to him in 1628, and that in conjunction with the Earl of St. Alban's he also received the dedication of Davenant's *Madagascar*.

Let there be patrons, etc. Burton, I. ii. 3, § 15. 'Tis an old saying: " Sint Mæcenates, non deerunt, Flacce, Marones " (Mart. VIII. lvi. 5).

Fabius, Cotta, and Lentulus are examples of Roman patrons of poetry, themselves distinguished. Cp. Juvenal, vii. 94.

119. *His tapers thus put out.* So Ovid, *Am.* iii. 9 :—

Ecce puer Veneris fert eversamque pharetram
Et fractos arcus, et sine luce facem.

121. *Four things make us happy here.* From

Ὑγιαίνειν μὲν ἄριστον ἀνδρὶ θνατῷ·
δεύτερον δὲ φυὰν καλὸν γενέσθαι·
τὸ τρίτον δὲ πλουτεῖν ἀδόλως·
καὶ τὸ τέταρτον, ἡβᾶν μετὰ τῶν φίλων.

(Bergk, *Anth. Lyr.*, *Scol.* 8.)

123. *The Tear sent to her from Staines.* This is printed in *Witts Recreations* with no other variation than in the title, which there runs: "A Teare sent his Mistresse". Dr. Grosart notes that Staines was at the time a royal residence.

128. *His Farewell to Sack.* A manuscript version of this poem at the British Museum omits many lines (7, 8, 11-22, 29-36), and contains few important variants. "Of the yet chaste and undefiled bride" is a poor anticipation of line 6, and "To raise the holy madness" for "To rouse the sacred madness" is also weak. For the line and a half:—

"Prithee not smile
Or smile more inly, lest thy looks beguile,"

we have the very inferior passage:—

"I prithee draw in
Thy gazing fires, lest at their sight the sin
Of fierce idolatry shoot into me, and
I turn apostate to the strict command
Of nature; bid me now farewell, or smile
More ugly, lest thy tempting looks beguile".

This MS. version is followed in the first published text in *Witts Recreations*, 1645.

130. *Upon Mrs. Eliz. Wheeler.* "The lady complimented in this poem was probably a relation by

marriage. Herrick's first cousin, Martha, the seventh daughter of his uncle Robert, married Mr. John Wheeler." Nott.

132. *Fold now thine arms.* A sign of grief. Cp. " His arms in this sad knot". *Tempest.*

134. *Mr. J. Warr.* This John Warr is probably the same as the " honoured friend, Mr. John Weare, Councellour," of a later poem. Dr. Grosart quotes an " Epitaph upon his honoured friend, Master Warre," by Randolph. Nothing is known of him, but I find in the Oxford Register that a John Warr matriculated at Exeter College, 16th May, 1619, and proceeded M.A. in 1624. He may possibly be Herrick's friend.

137. *Dowry with a wife.* Cp. Ovid, *Ars Am.* ii. 155 : Dos est uxoria lites.

139. *The Wounded Cupid.* This is taken from Anacreon, 33 [40] :—

Ἔρως ποτ' ἐν ῥόδοισιν ὄλωλα κἀποθνήσκω·
κοιμωμένην μέλιτταν ὄφις μ' ἔτυψε μικρός
οὐκ εἶδεν, ἀλλ' ἐτρώθη πτερωτός, ὃν καλοῦσιν
τὸν δάκτυλον· παταχθεὶς μέλιτταν οἱ γεωργοί.
τὰς χεῖρας ὠλόλυξεν· ἁ δ' εἶπεν· εἰ τὸ κέντρον
δραμὼν δὲ καὶ πετασθεὶς πονεῖ τὸ τᾶς μελίττας,
πρὸς τὴν καλὴν Κυθήρην πόσον δοκεῖς πονοῦσιν,
ὄλωλα, μᾶτερ, εἶπεν, Ἔρως, ὅσους σὺ βάλλεις;

142. *A Virgin's face she had.* Herrick is imitating a charming passage from the first Æneid (ll. 315-320), in which Æneas is confronted by Venus :—

Virginis os habitumque gerens et virginis arma,
Spartanae vel qualis equos Threissa fatigat
Harpalyce volucremque fuga praevertitur Eurum.

Namque umeris de more habilem suspenderat arcum
Venatrix, dederatque comam diffundere ventis,
Nuda genu nodoque sinus collecta fluentis.

With a wand of myrtle, etc. Cp. Anacreon, 7
[29]:—

> Ὑακινθίνῃ με ῥάβδῳ
> χαλέπως, Ἔρως ῥαπίζων . . . εἶπε ·
> Σὺ, γὰρ οὐ δύνῃ φιλῆσαι.

146. *Upon the Bishop of Lincoln's Imprisonment.*
John Williams (1582-1650), Bishop of Lincoln, 1621 ;
Lord Keeper of the Privy Seal, 1621-1625 ; suspended
and imprisoned, 1637-1640, on a frivolous charge of
having betrayed the king's secrets ; Archbishop of
York, 1641. Save from this poem and the *Carol*
printed in the Appendix we know nothing of his relations with Herrick. He had probably stood in the
way of the poet's obtaining holy orders or preferment.
When Herrick was appointed to the cure of Dean Prior
in 1629, Williams had already lost favour at the Court.

147. *Cynthius pluck ye by the ear.* Cp. Virg. *Ecl.*
vi. 3 : Cynthius aurem Vellit et admonuit; and
Milton's *Lycidas,* 77 : " Phœbus replied and touched
my trembling ears ".

The lazy man the most doth love. Cp. Ovid,
Remed. Amor. 144: Cedit amor rebus: res age,
tutus eris. Nott. But Ovid could also write :
Qui nolet fieri desidiosus amet (1 *Am.* ix. 46).

149. *Sir Thomas Southwell,* of Hangleton, Sussex,
knighted 1615, died before December 16, 1642.

Those tapers five. Mentioned by Plutarch, *Qu.
Rom.* 2. For their significance see Ben Jonson's
Masque of Hymen.

O'er the threshold force her in. The custom of lifting the bride over the threshold, probably to avert an ill-omened stumble, has prevailed among the most diverse races. For the anointing of the doorposts Brand quotes Langley's translation of Polydore Vergil : " The bryde anoynted the poostes of the doores with swynes' grease, because she thought by that meanes to dryve awaye all misfortune, whereof she had her name in Latin ' Uxor ab unguendo ' ".

To gather nuts. A Roman marriage custom mentioned in Catullus, *Carm.* lxi. 124-127, the *In Nuptias Juliæ et Manlii,* which Herrick keeps in mind all through this ode.

With all lucky birds to side. Bona cum bona nubit alite virgo. Cat. *Carm.* lxi. 18.

But when ye both can say Come. The wish in this case appears to have been fulfilled, as Lady Southwell administered to her husband's estate, Dec. 16, 1642, and her own estate was administered on the thirtieth of the following January.

Two ripe shocks of corn. Cp. Job v. 26.

153. *His wish.* From Hor. *Epist.* I. xviii. 111, 112 :—

Sed satis est orare Jovem quæ donat et aufert ;
Det vitam, det opes ; æquum mî animum ipse parabo :

where Herrick seems to have read *qui* for *quæ.*

157. *No Herbs have power to cure Love.* Ovid, *Met.* i. 523 ; id. *Her.* v. 149 : Nullis amor est medicabilis herbis. For the 'only one sovereign salve' cp. Seneca, *Hippol.* 1189 : Mors amoris una sedamen.

159. *The Cruel Maid.* Printed in *Witts Recreations*, 1650, with no other variant than the mistaken omission of "how" in l. 7. I do not think that it has been yet pointed out that the whole poem is a close imitation of Theocritus, xxiii. 19-47 :—

Ἄγριε παῖ καὶ στυγνέ, κ.τ.λ.

Possibly Herrick meant to translate the whole poem, which would explain his initial *And.* But cp. Ben Jonson's *Engl. Gram.* ch. viii.: "'And' in the beginning of a sentence serveth instead of an admiration".

164. *To a Gentlewoman objecting to him his gray hairs.* Mr. Hazlitt quotes an early MS. copy headed: "An old man to his younge Mrs.". The variants, as he observes, are mostly for the worse. The poem may have been suggested to Herrick by Anacreon, 6 [11]:—

Λέγουσιν αἱ γυναῖκες,
'Ανακρέων, γέρων εἶ ·
λαβὼν ἔσοπτρον ἄθρει
κόμας μὲν οὐκέτ' οὔσας κ.τ.λ.

168. *Jos. Lo. Bishop of Exeter.* Joseph Hall, 1574-1656, author of the satires.

169. *The Countess of Carlisle.* Lucy, the second wife of James, first Earl of Carlisle, the Lady Carlisle of Browning's *Strafford.*

170. *I fear no earthly powers.* Probably suggested by Anacreon [36], beginning: τί με τοὺς νόμους διδάσκεις; Cp. also 7 [15]: Οὔ μοι μέλει τὰ Γύγεω.

172. *A Ring presented to Julia.* Printed without variation in *Witts Recreations*, 1650, under the title: "With a ◎ to Julia ".

174. *Still thou reply'st: The Dead.* Cp. Martial, VIII. lxix. 1, 2 :—

> Miraris veteres, Vacerra, solos
> Nec laudas nisi mortuos poetas.

178. *Corinna's going a-Maying.* Herrick's poem is a charming expansion of Chaucer's theme : " For May wol have no slogardye a night ". The account of May-day customs in Brand (vol. i. pp. 212-234) is unusually full, and all Herrick's allusions can be illustrated from it. Dr. Nott compares the last stanza to Catullus, *Carm.* v. ; but parallels from the classic poets could be multiplied indefinitely.

The God unshorn of l. 2 is from Hor. I. *Od.* xxi. 2 : Intonsum pueri dicite Cynthium.

181. *A dialogue between Horace and Lydia.* Hor. III. *Od.* ix.

Ramsey. Organist of Trinity College, Cambridge, 1628-1634. Some of his music still exists in MS.

185. *An Ode to Master Endymion Porter, upon his brother's death.* Endymion Porter is said to have had an only brother, Giles, who died in the king's service at Oxford, *i.e.*, between 1642 and 1646, and it has been taken for granted that this ode refers to his death. The supposition is possibly right, but if so, the ode, despite its beauty, is so gratingly and extraordinarily selfish that we may wonder if the dead brother is not the William Herrick of the next poem. The first verse is, of course, a soliloquy of Herrick's, not, as Dr. Grosart suggests, addressed to him by Porter. Dr. Nott again parallels Catullus, *Carm.* v.

186. *To his dying brother, Master William Herrick.* According to Dr. Grosart and Mr. Hazlitt the

18

poet had an elder brother, William, baptized at St. Vedast's, Foster Lane, Nov. 24, 1585 (he must have been born some months earlier, if this date be right, for his sister Martha was baptized in the following January), and alive in 1629, when he acted as one of the executors of his mother's will. But, it is said, there was also another brother named William, born in 1593, after his father's death, " at Harry Campion's house at Hampton ". I have not been able to find the authority for this last statement, which, as it asserts the co-existence of two brothers, of the same name, is certainly surprising. According to Dr. Grosart, it is the younger William who "died young" and was addressed in this poem, but I must own to feeling some doubt in the matter.

193. *The Lily in a Crystal.* The poem may be taken as an expansion of Martial, VIII. lxviii. 5-8 :—

Condita perspicuâ vivit vindemia gemmâ
   Et tegitur felix, nec tamen uva latet :
Femineum lucet sic per bombycina corpus,
   Calculus in nitidâ sic numeratur aquâ.

197. *The Welcome to Sack.* Two MSS. at the British Museum (Harl. 6931 and Add. 19,268) contain copies of this important poem. These copies differ considerably from the printed version, are proved by small variations to be independent of each other, and at the same time agree in all important points. We may conclude, therefore, that they represent an earlier version of the poem, subsequently revised by Herrick before the issue of *Hesperides*. In the subjoined copy, in which the two MSS. are corrected

from each other, italics show the variations, asterisks
mark lines omitted in *Hesperides*, and a dagger the
absence of lines subsequently added.

" So *swift* streams meet, so springs with gladder
    smiles
Meet after long divorcement *made by* isles:
When love (the child of likeness) urgeth on
Their crystal *waters* to an union.
So meet stol'n kisses when the moonie *night*
Calls forth fierce lovers to their wisht *delight:*
So kings and queens meet, when desire convinces
All thoughts, *save those that tend to* getting princes.
As I meet thee, Soul of my life and fame!
Eternal Lamp of Love, whose radiant flame
Out-*darts* the heaven's Osiris; and thy *gems*
Darken the splendour of his mid-day beams.
Welcome, O welcome, my illustrious spouse!
Welcome as are the ends unto my vows:
Nay, far more welcome than the happy soil
The sea-scourged merchant, after all his toil,
Salutes with tears of joy, when fires *display*
The *smoking* chimneys of his Ithaca.
Where hast thou been so long from my embraces,
Poor pitied exile? Tell me, did thy Graces
Fly discontented hence, and for a time
Choose rather for to bless *some* other clime?
†* *Oh, then, not longer let my sweet defer*
* *Her buxom smiles from me, her worshipper!*
Why *have those amber* looks, the which have been
Time-past so fragrant, sickly now *call'd in*
Like a dull twilight? Tell me, * *hath my soul*

* *Prophaned in speech or done an act that is foul*
* *Against thy purer essence ?   For that* fault
I'll expiate with sulphur, hair and salt :
And with the crystal humour of the spring
Purge hence the guilt, and kill *the* quarrelling.
Wilt thou not smile, *nor* tell me what's amiss ?
Have I been cold to hug thee, too remiss,
Too temperate in embracing ?   Tell me, has desire
To-thee-ward died in the embers, and no fire
Left in *the* raked-up *ashes*, as a mark
To testify the glowing of a spark ?
†*I must* confess I left thee, and appeal
'Twas done by me more to *increase* my zeal,
And double my affection[†]; as do those
Whose love grows more inflamed by being *froze*.
But to forsake thee, [†] could there *ever* be
A thought of such-like possibility ?
When *all the world may know that vines* shall lack
Grapes, before Herrick *leave* Canary sack.
**Sack is my life, my leaven, salt to all*
**My dearest dainties, nay, 'tis the principal*
**Fire unto all my functions, gives me blood,*
**An active spirit, full marrow, and, what is good,*
Sack makes me *sprightful, airy* to be borne,
Like Iphyclus, upon the tops of corn.
Sack makes me nimble, as the wingèd hours,
To dance and caper *o'er the tops* of flowers,
And ride the sunbeams.   Can there be a thing
Under the *cope of heaven* that can bring
More *joy* unto my *soul*, or can present
My Genius with a fuller blandishment ?
Illustrious Idol !   *Can* the Egyptians seek

Help from the garlick, onion and the leek,
And pay no vows to thee, who *art the* best
God, and far more *transcending* than the rest?
Had Cassius, that weak water-drinker, known
Thee in *the* Vine, or had but tasted one
Small chalice of thy *nectar, he, even* he
As the wise Cato had approved of thee.
Had not Jove's son, the *rash* Tyrinthian swain
(Invited to the Thesbian banquet), ta'ne
Full goblets of thy [†] blood; his **lustful* sprite
Had not kept heat for fifty maids that night.
†As Queens meet Queens, *so let sack come to* me
Or as Cleopatra *unto* Anthonie,
When her high *visage* did at once present
To the Triumvir love and wonderment.
Swell up my *feeble sinews*, let my blood
†Fill each part full of fire,* *let all my good*
Parts be encouraged, active to do
What thy commanding soul shall put *me* to,
And till I turn apostate to thy love,
Which here I vow to serve, *never* remove
Thy *blessing* from me; but Apollo's curse
Blast *all mine* actions; or, a thing that's worse,
When these circumstants *have the fate* to see
The time *when* I prevaricate from thee,
Call me the Son of Beer, and then confine
Me to the tap, the toast, the turf; let wine
Ne'er shine upon me; *let* my *verses* all
Haste to a sudden death and funeral:
And last, *dear Spouse, when I thee* disavow,
May ne'er prophetic Daphne crown my brow."

 Certainly this manuscript version is in every way

inferior to that printed in the *Hesperides*, and Herrick must be reckoned among the poets who are
able to revise their own work.

The smoky chimneys of his Ithaca. Ovid, I. *de
Ponto*, ix. 265 :—

> Non dubia est Ithaci prudentia sed tamen optat
>   Fumum de patriis posse videre focis.

Upon the tops of corn. Virgil (*Æn.* vii. 808-9)
uses the same comparison of Camilla : Illa vel
intactae segetis per summa volaret Gramina, nec
teneras cursu laesisset aristas.

*Could the Egyptians seek Help from the garlick,
onion and the leek.* Cp. Numbers xi. 5, and Juv.,
xi. 9-11.

Cassius, that weak water-drinker. Not, as Dr.
Grosart queries : " Cassius Iatrosophista, or Cassius
Felix ? " but C. Cassius Longinus, the murderer of
Cæsar. Cp. Montaigne, II. 2, and Seneca, *Ep.* 83 :
" Cassius totâ vitâ aquam bibit " there quoted.

201. *To trust to good verses.* Carminibus con-
fide bonis. Ovid, *Am.* III. ix. 39.

The Golden Pomp is come. Aurea pompa venit,
Ovid, *Am.* III. ii. 44. " Now reigns the rose " (nunc
regnat rosa) is a common phrase in Martial and
elsewhere. For the "Arabian dew," cp. Ovid, *Sappho
to Phaon*, 98 : Arabo noster rore capillus olet.

A text . . . Behold Tibullus lies. Jacet ecce
Tibullus : Vix manet e tanto parva quod urna capit.
Ovid, *Am.* III. ix. 39.

203. *Lips Tongueless.* Dr. Nott parallels Catullus,
Carm. lii. (lv.) :—

Si linguam clauso tenes in ore,
Fructus projicies amoris omnes :
Verbosa gaudet Venus loquela.

208. *Gather ye rosebuds while ye may.* Set to
music by William Lawes in Playford's second book
of "Ayres," 1652. Printed in *Witts Recreations,*
1654, with the variants : " Gather *your* Rosebuds "
in l. 1 ; l. 4, *may* for *will;* l. 6, *he is getting* for
he's a-getting; l. 8, *nearer to his setting* for *nearer
he's to setting.* The opening lines are from Ausonius,
ccclxi. 49, 50 (quoted by Burton, *Anat. Mel.* III. 2,
5 § 5) :—

Collige, virgo, rosas, dum flos novus, et nova pubes,
    Et memor esto aevum sic properare tuum :

cp. also l. 43 :—

Quam longa una dies, ætas tam longa rosarum.

209. *Has not whence to sink at all.* Seneca, *Ep.*
xx. : Redige te ad parva ex quibus cadere non possis.
Cp. Alain Delisle : Qui decumbit humi non habet unde
cadat.

211. *His poetry his pillar.* A variation upon the
Horatian theme :—

    " Exegi monumentum aere perennius
        Regalique situ pyramidum altius ".
                                (III. *Od.* xxx.)

212. *What though the sea be calm.* Almost literally translated from Seneca, *Ep.* iv. : Noli huic tran-
quillitati confidere : momento mare evertitur : eodem
die ubi luserunt navigia sorbentur.

213. *At noon of day was seen a silver star.* " King
Charles the First went to St. Paul's Church the 30th
day of May, 1630, to give praise for the birth of his
son, attended with all his Peers and a most royal
Train, where a bright star appeared at High Noon
in the sight of all." (*Stella Meridiana*, 1661.)

213. *And all most sweet, yet all less sweet than he.*
It is characteristic of Herrick' that in his *Noble
Numbers* (" The New-Year's Gift ") he repeats this
line, applying it to Christ.

The swiftest grace is best. Ὠκεῖαι χάριτες γλυκερώ-
τεραι. Anth. Pal. x. 30.

214. *Know thy when.* So in *The Star-song* Herrick sings : " Thou canst clear All doubts and manifest
the where ".

219. *Lord Bernard Stewart,* fourth son of Esme,
third Duke of Lennox, and himself created Earl of
Lichfield by Charles I. He commanded the king's
troop of guards, and was killed at the battle of
Rowton Heath, outside Chester, Sept. 24, 1645.

Clarendon (*History of the Rebellion*, ix. 19) thus
records his death and character : " Here fell many
gentlemen and officers of name, with the brave Earl
of Litchfield, who was the third brother of that
illustrious family that sacrificed his life in this
quarrel. He was a very faultless young man, of a
most gentle, courteous, and affable nature, and of
a spirit and courage invincible ; whose loss all men
lamented, and the king bore it with extraordinary
grief."

Trentall. Properly a set of thirty masses for the
repose of a dead man's soul. Here and elsewhere

Herrick uses the word as an equivalent for dirge, but Sidney distinguished them : "Let dirige be sung and trentalls rightly read. For love is dead," etc. "Hence, hence profane," is the Latin, *procul o procul este profani* of Virg. *Æn.* vi. 258, where "profane" is only equivalent to uninitiated.

223. *The Fairy Temple.* For a brief note on Herrick's fairy poems, see Appendix. On the dedication to Mr. John, Merrifield, Counsellor-at-Law, Dr. Grosart remarks : "Nothing seems to be now known of Merrifield. It is just possible that—as throughout the poem—the name was an invented one, 'Merry Field'." But the records of the Inner Temple show that the Merrifields were a legal family from Woolmiston, near Crewkerne, Somersetshire. John (son of Richard) Merrifield, the father, was admitted to the Inner Temple in 1581, and John, the son, in 1611. This latter must be Herrick's Counsellor. He rose to be a Master of the Bench in 1638 and Sergeant-at-Law in 1660. He died October, 1666, aged 75, at Crewkerne. On the other hand, it can hardly be doubted that Dr. Grosart is right in regarding the names of the fairy saints as quite imaginary. He nevertheless suggests SS. Titus, Neot, Idus, Ida, Fridian or Fridolin, Trypho, Felan and Felix as the possible prototypes of "Saint *Tit*, Saint *Nit*, Saint *Is*," etc. It should be noted that "Tit and Nit" occur with "Wap and Win" and other obviously made-up names, in Drayton's *Nymphidia.*

229. *Upon Cupid.* Taken from Anacreon, 5 [59].

Στέφος πλέκων ποθ' εὗρον
ἐν τοῖς ῥόδοις Ἔρωτα·

καὶ τῶν πτερῶν κατασχών
ἐβάπτισ' εἰς τὸν οἶνον ·
λαβὼν δ' ἔπινον αὐτόν,
καὶ νῦν ἔσω μελῶν μου
πτεροῖσι γαργαλίζει.

234. *Care will make a face.* Ovid, *Ar. Am.* iii.
105 : Cura dabit faciem, facies neglecta peribit.

235. *Upon Himself.* Printed in *Witts Recreations,*
1654, under the title : *On an old Batchelor,* and with
the variants, *married* for *wedded,* l. 3, *one* for *a* in l.
4, and *Rather than mend me, blind me quite* in l. 6.

238. *To the Rose.* Printed in *Witts Recreations,*
1654, with the variants *peevish* for *flowing* in l. 4,
say, if she frets, that I have bonds in l. 6, *that can
tame although not kill* in l. 10, and *now* for *thus* in
l. 11. The opening couplet is from Martial, VII.
lxxxix. :—

I, felix rosa, mollibusque sertis
Nostri cinge comas Apollinaris.

241. *Upon a painted Gentlewoman.* Printed in
Witts Recreations, 1650, under the title, *On a
painted madame.*

250. *Mildmay, Earl of Westmoreland.* See Note
to 112. According to the date of the earl's succession, this poem must have been written after
1628.

253. *He that will not love,* etc. Ovid, *Rem. Am.*
15, 16 :—

Si quis male fert indignae regna puellae,
Ne pereat nostrae sentiat artis opem.

How she is her own least part. *Ib.* 344 : Pars minima est ipsa puella sui, quoted by Bacon, Burton, Lyly, and Montaigne.

Printed in *Witts Recreations*, 1654, with the variants, '*freezing* colds and *fiery* heats,' and 'and how she is *in every* part '.

256. *Had Lesbia*, etc. See Catullus, *Carm.* iii.

260. *How violets came blue.* Printed in *Witts Recreations*, 1654, as *How the violets came blue.* The first two lines read :—

" The violets, as poets tell,
With Venus wrangling went ".

Other variants are *did* for *sho'd* in l. 3 ; *Girl* for *Girls ; you* for *ye ; do* for *dare.*

264. *That verse*, etc. Herrick repeats this assurance in a different context in the second of his *Noble Numbers, His Prayer for Absolution.*

269. *The Gods to Kings the judgment give to sway.* From Tacitus, *Ann.* vi. 8 (M. Terentius to Tiberius): Tibi summum rerum judicium dii dedere ; nobis obsequi gloria relicta est.

270. *He that may sin, sins least.* Ovid, *Amor.* III. iv. 9, 10 :—

Cui peccare licet, peccat minus : ipsa potestas
Semina nequitiae languidiora facit.

271. *Upon a maid that died the day she was married.* Cp. Meleager, Anth. Pal. vii. 182 :

Οὐ γάμον ἀλλ' Ἀΐδαν ἐπινυμφίδιον Κλεαρίστα
δέξατο παρθενίας ἅμματα λυομένα ·
Ἄρτι γὰρ ἑσπέριοι νύμφας ἐπὶ δικλίσιν ἄχευν
λωτοί, καὶ θαλάμων ἐπλαταγεῦντο θύραι ·

'Ηῷοι δ' ὀλολυγμὸν ἀνέκραγον, ἐκ δ' Ὑμέναιος
σιγαθεὶς γοερὸν φθέγμα μεθαρμόσατο,
Αἱ δ' αὐταὶ καὶ φέγγος ἐδᾳδούχουν παρὰ παστῷ
πεῦκαι καὶ φθιμένᾳ νέρθεν ἔφαινον ὁδόν.

278. *To his Household Gods.* Obviously written
at the time of his ejection from his living.

283. *A Nuptial Song on Sir Clipseby Crew.* Of
this Epithalamium (written in 1625 for the marriage
of Sir Clipseby Crew, knighted by James I. at Theo-
bald's in 1620, with Jane, daughter of Sir John
Pulteney), two manuscript versions, substantially
agreeing, are preserved at the British Museum (Harl.
MS. 6917, and Add. 25, 303). Seven verses are
transcribed in these manuscripts which Herrick
afterwards saw fit to omit, and almost every verse
contains variants of importance. It is impossible
to convey the effect of the earlier version by a mere
collation, and I therefore transcribe it in full, despite
its length. As before, variants and additions are
printed in italics. The numbers in brackets are
those of the later version, as given in *Hesperides.*
The marginal readings are variants of Add. 25, 303,
from the Harleian manuscript.

1 [1].

" What's that we see from far ? the spring of Day
Bloom'd from the East, or fair *enamell'd* May
　　Blown out of April; or some new
　　Star fill'd with glory to our view,
　　　　Reaching at Heaven,
To add a nobler Planet to the seven ?
　　Say or do we not descry

Some Goddess in a Cloud of Tiffany
　　To move, or rather the
Emerg*ing* Venus from the sea?

2 [2].

" 'Tis she! 'tis she! or else some more Divine
Enlightened substance; mark how from the shrine
　　Of holy Saints she paces on
　　Throwing about Vermilion
　　　And Amber: spice-
ing the chafte-air with fumes of Paradise.
　　Then come on, come on, and yield
A savour like unto a blessed field,
　　When the bedabbled morn
　　Washes the golden ears of corn.

3.

" Lead on fair paranymphs, the while her eyes,
Guilty of somewhat, ripe the strawberries
　　And cherries in her cheeks, there's cream
　　Already spilt, her rays must gleam
　　　Gently thereon,
And so beget lust and temptation
　　To surfeit and to hunger.
Help on her pace; and, though she lag, yet stir
　　Her homewards; well she knows
Her heart's at home, howe'er she goes.

4 [3].

" See where she comes; and smell how all the street
Breathes Vine-yards and Pomegranates: O how sweet,

As a fir'd Altar, is each stone
Spirting forth pounded Cinnamon.
    The Phœnix nest,
Built up of odours, burneth in her breast.
    Who *would not then* consume
His soul to *ashes* in that rich perfume ?   [ash-heaps
        Bestroking Fate the while
    He burns to embers on the Pile.

5 [4].

" Hymen, O Hymen ! tread the sacred *round* [ground
Shew thy white feet, and head with Marjoram
        crowned :
    Mount up thy flames, and let thy Torch
    Display *thy* Bridegroom in the porch
        In his desires
More towering, more *besparkling* than thy fires :
    Shew her how his eyes do turn   [disparkling
And roll about, and in their motions burn
        Their balls to cinders : haste
    Or, *like a firebrand*, he will waste.

6.

" *See how he waves his hand, and through his eyes*
Shoots forth his jealous soul, for to surprise
    And ravish you his Bride, do you
    Not now perceive the soul of C[lipseby] C[rew],
        Your mayden knight,
            With kisses to inspire
    You with his just and holy ire.

7 [5].

"*If so, glide through the ranks of Virgins*, pass
The Showers of Roses, lucky four-leaved grass :
    The while the cloud of younglings sing,
    And drown *you* with a flowery spring :
        While some repeat
Your praise, and bless you, sprinkling you with
    Wheat,
    While that others do divine,
' Blest is the Bride on whom the Sun doth shine ' ;
        And thousands gladly wish
    You multiply as *do the* fish.

8.

"*Why then go forward, sweet Auspicious Bride,*
And come upon your Bridegroom like a Tide
    Bearing down Time before you ; hye
    Swell, mix, and loose your souls ; imply
        Like streams which flow
Encurled together, and no difference show
    In their [most] silver waters ; run
Into your selves like wool together spun,
        Or blend so as the sight
    Of two makes one Hermaphrodite.

9 [6].

" And, beauteous Bride, we do confess *you* are wise
On drawing forth *those* bashful jealousies   [doling
    In love's name, do so ; and a price
    Set on yourself by being nice.

But yet take heed.
What now you seem be not the same indeed,
    And turn Apostat*a* : Love will
Part of the way be met, or sit stone still ;
        On them, and though *y'are slow*
    In going yet, howsoever go.

10.

" *How long, soft Bride, shall your dear C[lipseby] make*
Love to your welcome with the mystic cake,
    How long, oh pardon, shall the house
    And the smooth Handmaids pay their vows
        With oil and wine
For your approach, yet see their Altars pine ?
        How long shall the page to please
You stand for to surrender up the keys
        Of the glad house ?   Come, come,
    Or Lar will freeze to death at home.

11.

" *Welcome at last unto the Threshold, Time*
Throned in a saffron evening, seems to chime
    All in, kiss and so enter.   If
    A prayer must be said, be brief,
        The easy Gods
For such neglect have only myrtle rods
    To stroke, not strike ; fear you
Not more, mild Nymph, than they would have you do ;
        But dread that you do more offend
    In that you do begin than end.

12 [7].

"And now y'are entered, see the coddled cook
Runs from his Torrid Zone to pry and look
    And bless his dainty mistress ; see
    How th' aged point out : ' This is she
        Who now must sway
Us (*and God* shield her) with her yea and nay,'
    And the smirk Butler thinks it
Sin in *his* nap'ry not t' express his wit ;
        Each striving to devise
    Some gin wherewith to catch *her* eyes.

13.

" *What though your laden Altar now has won*
The credit from the table of the Sun
    For earth and sea ; this cost
    On you is altogether lost
        Because you feed
Not on the flesh of beasts, but on the seed
    Of contemplation : your,
Your eyes are they, wherewith you draw the pure
        Elixir to the mind
    Which sees the body fed, yet pined.

14 [14].

" If *you must needs* for ceremonie's sake
Bless a sack posset, Luck go with *you,* take
    The night charm quickly ; you have spells
    And magic for to end, and Hells
        To pass, but such

19

And of such torture as no *God* would grutch
    To live therein for ever: fry,
Aye and consume, and grow again to die,
    And live, and in that case
      Love the *damnation* of *that* place.   [the

15 [8].

" To Bed, to Bed, *sweet* Turtles now, and write
This the shortest day,† this the longest night
    And yet too short for you; 'tis we
    Who count this night as long as three,
      Lying alone
Hearing the clock *go* Ten, Eleven, Twelve, One:
    Quickly, quickly then prepare,
And let the young men and the Bridemaids share
    Your garters, and their joints
    Encircle with the Bridegroom's points.

16 [9].

" By the Bride's eyes, and by the teeming life
Of her green hopes, we charge you that no strife,
    Further than *virtue lends*, gets place
    Among *you catching at* her Lace.
      Oh, do not fall
Foul in these noble pastimes, lest you call
    Discord in, and so divide
The *gentle* Bridegroom and the *fragrous* Bride,
    Which Love forefend: but spoken
    Be't to your praise: ' No peace was broken '.

17 [10].

" Strip her of spring-time, tender whimpering maids,
Now Autumn's come, when all *those* flowery aids
    Of her delays must end, dispose
    That Lady-smock, that pansy and that Rose
        Neatly apart;
But for prick-madam, and for gentle-heart,
    And soft maiden-blush, the Bride
Makes holy these, all others lay aside :
    Then strip her, or unto her
    Let him come who dares undo her.

18 [11].

" And to enchant *you* more, *view* everywhere   [ye
About the roof a Syren in a sphere,
    As we think, singing to the din
    Of many a warbling cherubin :
        List, oh list! how
Even heaven gives up his soul between you now, [ye
    Mark how thousand Cupids fly
To light their Tapers at the Bride's bright eye ;
    To bed, or her they'll tire,
    Were she an element of fire.

19 [12].

" And to your more bewitching, see the proud
Plump bed bear up, and *rising* like a cloud,
    Tempting *thee, too, too* modest ; can
    You see it brussle like a swan
        And you be cold

To meet it, when it woos and seems to fold
    The arms to hug *you ?* throw, throw
Yourselves into *that main, in the full* flow
      Of *the* white pride, and drown
    The *stars* with you in floods of down.

20 [13].

" *You see 'tis* ready, and the maze of love
Looks for the treaders ; everywhere is wove
    Wit and new mystery, read and
    Put in practice, to understand
      And know each wile,
Each Hieroglyphic of a kiss or smile ;
    And do it *in* the full, reach
High in your own conceipts, and *rather* teach
      Nature and Art one more
    Sport than they ever knew before.

21.

To the Maidens :]
" *And now y' have wept enough, depart ; yon stars* [the
Begin to pink, as weary that the wars
    Know so long Treaties ; beat the Drum
    Aloft, and like two armies, come
      And guild the field,
Fight bravely for the flame of mankind, yield
    Not to this, or that assault,
For that would prove more Heresy than fault
      In combatants to fly
    'Fore this or that hath got the victory.

22 [15].

"But since it must be done, despatch and sew
Up in a sheet your Bride, and what if so
    It be with *rib of Rock and* Brass,
    Yea tower her up, as Danae was,   [ye
        Think you that this,
Or Hell itself, a powerful Bulwark is?
    I tell *you* no; but like a   [ye
Bold bolt of thunder he will make his way,
    And rend the cloud, and throw
    The sheet about, like flakes of snow.

23 [16].

"All now is hushed in silence: Midwife-moon
With all her Owl-ey'd issue begs a boon
    Which you must grant; that's entrance with
    Which extract, all we † call pith
        And quintessence
Of Planetary bodies; so commence,
    All fair constellations
Looking upon *you*, that *the* Nations
        Springing from to such Fires
    May blaze the virtue of their Sires."
                —R. Herrick.

The variants in this version are not very important; one of the most noteworthy, *round* for *ground*, in stanza 5 [4], was overlooked by Dr. Grosart in his collation. Of the seven stanzas subsequently omitted several are of great beauty. There are few happier images in Herrick than that of *Time throned in a saffron evening* in stanza 11. It is only when the earlier version is read as a whole that Herrick's taste in omitting is vindicated. Each stanza is good in itself, but in the MSS. the poem drags from excessive length, and the reduction of its twenty-three stanzas to sixteen greatly improves it.

286. *Ever full of pensive fear.* Ovid, *Heroid.* i. 12: Res est solliciti plena timoris amor.

287. *Reverence to riches.* Perhaps from Tacit. *Ann.* ii. 33: Neque in familia et argento quæque ad usum parantur nimium aliquid aut modicum, nisi ex fortuna possidentis.

288. *Who forms a godhead.* From Martial, VIII. xxiv. 5 :—

Qui fingit sacros auro vel marmore vultus
　　Non facit ille deos : qui rogat, ille facit.

290. *The eyes be first that conquered are.* From Tacitus, *Germ.* 43 : Primi in omnibus proeliis oculi vincuntur.

293. *Oberon's Feast.* For a note on Herrick's Fairy Poems and on the *Description of the King and Queene of the Fayries* (1635), in which part of this poem was first printed, see Appendix. Add. MS. 22, 603, at the British Museum, and Ashmole MS. 38, at the Bodleian, contain early versions of the poem substantially agreeing. I transcribe the Museum copy :—

" A little mushroom table spread
After *the dance*, they set on bread,
A *yellow corn of hecky* wheat
With some small *sandy* grit to eat

His choice bits; with *which* in a trice
They make a feast less great than nice.
But all *the* while his eye *was* served
We *dare* not think his ear was sterved:
But that there was in place to stir
His *fire* the *pittering* Grasshopper;
The merry Cricket, puling Fly,
The piping Gnat for minstralcy.
The Humming Dor, the dying Swan,
And each a choice Musician.
And now we must imagine first,
The Elves present to quench his thirst
A pure seed-pearl of infant dew,
Brought and *beswetted* in a blue
And pregnant violet; which done,
His kitling eyes begin to run
Quite through the table, where he spies
The horns of papery Butterflies:
Of which he eats, *but with* a little
Neat cool allay of Cuckoo's spittle;
A little Fuz-ball pudding stands
By, yet not blessed by his hands—
That was too coarse, but *he not spares*
To feed upon the candid hairs
Of a dried canker, with a sagg
And well *bestuffed* Bee's sweet bag:
Stroking his pallet with some store
Of Emme*t* eggs.   What would he more,
But Beards of Mice, *an Ewt's* stew'd thigh,
A pickled maggot and a dry
Hipp, with a Red cap worm, that's shut
Within the concave of a Nut

Brown as his tooth, *and with the fat*
And well-boiled inchpin of a Bat.
A bloated Earwig with the Pith
Of sugared rush aglads him with ;
But most of all the Glow-worm's fire,
As most betickling his desire
To know his Queen, mixt with the far-
Fetcht binding-jelly of a star.
The silk-worm's seed, a little moth
Lately fattened in a piece of cloth ;
Withered cherries ; Mandrake's ears ;
Mole's eyes ; to these the slain stag's tears ;
The unctuous dewlaps of a Snail ;
The broke heart of a Nightingale
O'er-come in music ; with a wine
Ne'er ravished from the flattering Vine,
But gently pressed from the soft side
Of the most sweet and dainty Bride,
Brought in a *daisy chalice*, which
He fully quaffs *off* to bewitch
His blood *too high*.　This done, commended
Grace by his Priest, the feast is ended."

The Shapcott to whom this *Oberon's Feast* and
Oberon's Palace are dedicated is Herrick's " peculiar
friend, Master Thomas Shapcott, Lawyer," of a
later poem.　Dr. Grosart again suggests that it
may have been a character-name, but, as in the case
of John Merrifield, the owner was a West country-
man and a member of the Inner Temple, where
he was admitted in 1632 as the "son and heir of
Thomas Shapcott," of Exeter.

298. *That man lives twice.* From Martial, X. xxiii. 7 :—

> Ampliat aetatis spatium sibi vir bonus : hoc est
> Vivere bis vita posse priore frui.

301. *Master Edward Norgate, Clerk of the Signet of his Majesty :—*

Son to Robert Norgate, D.D., Master of Bene't College, Cambridge.   He was employed by the Earl of Arundel to purchase pictures, and on one occasion found himself at Marseilles without re-mittances, and had to tramp through France on foot.   According to the Calendars of State Papers in 1625, it was ordered that, "forasmuch as his Majesty's letters to the Grand Signior, the King of Persia, the Emperor of Russia, the Great Mogul, and other remote Princes, had been written, limned, and garnished with gold and colours by scriveners abroad, thenceforth they should be so written, limned, and garnished by Edward Norgate, Clerk of the Signet in reversion".   Six years later this order was renewed, the "Kings of Bantam, Macassar, Barbary, Siam, Achine, Fez, and Sus" being added to the previous list, and Norgate being now desig-nated as a Clerk of the Signet Extraordinary.   In the same year, having previously been Bluemantle Pursuivant, he was promoted to be Windsor Herald, in which capacity he received numerous fees during the next few years, and was excused ship money. He still, however, retained his clerkship, for he writes in 1639 : "The poor Office of Arms is fain to blazon the Council books and Signet".   The phrase

occurs in a series of nineteen letters of extraordinary
interest, which Norgate wrote from the North,
chiefly to his friend, Robert Reade, secretary to
Windebank, on the course of affairs.   In Sept., 1641,
"Ned Norgate" was ordered personally to attend
the king.   "It is his Majesty's pleasure that the
master should wait and not the men, and *that* they
shall find."   Henceforth I find no certain reference
to him; according to Fuller he died at the Herald's
Office in 1649.   It would be interesting if we could
be sure that this Edward Norgate is the same as
the one who in 1611 was appointed Tuner of his
Majesty's "virginals, organs, and other instruments,"
and in 1637 received a grant of £140 for the repair
of the organ at Hampton Court.   Herrick's love of
music makes us expect to find a similar trait in his
friends.

313. *The Entertainment, or Porch Verse.*   The
words *Ye wrong the threshold-god* and the allusion to
the porch in the Clipsby Crew Epithalamium (stanza
4) show that there is no reference here (as Brand
thinks, ii. 135) to the old custom of reading part of
the marriage service at the church door or porch (cp.
Chaucer: "Husbands at churchë door she had had
five").   The porch of the house is meant, and the
allusions are to the ceremonies at the threshold (cp.
the Southwell Epithalamium).   Dr. Grosart quotes
from the Dean Prior register the entry of the marriage of Henry Northleigh, gentleman, and Mistress
Lettice Yard on September 5, 1639, by licence from
the Archbishop of Canterbury.

319. *No noise of late-spawned Tittyries.*   In the

Camden Society's edition of the *Diary of Walter Yonge*, p. 70 (kindly shown me by the Rev. J. H. Ward), we have a contemporary account of the Club known as the Tityre Tues, which took its name from the first words of Virgil's first *Eclogue.* "The beginning of December, 1623, there was a great number in London, haunting taverns and other debauched places, who swore themselves in a brotherhood and named themselves *Tityre Tues.* The oath they gave in this manner: he that was to be sworn did put his dagger into a pottle of wine, and held his hand upon the pommel thereof, and then was to make oath that he would aid and assist all other of his fellowship and not disclose their council. There were divers knights, some young noblemen and gentlemen of this brotherhood, and they were to know one the other by a black bugle which they wore, and their followers to be known by a blue ribbond. There are discovered of them about 80 or 100 persons, and have been examined by the Privy Council, but nothing discovered of any intent they had. It is said that the king hath given commandment that they shall be re-examined." In Mennis's *Musarum Deliciæ* the brotherhood is celebrated in a poem headed "The Tytre Tues; or, a Mocke Song. To the tune of Chive Chase. By Mr. George Chambers." The second verse runs :—

> " They call themselves the Tytere-tues,
>   And wore a blue rib-bin ;
> And when a-drie would not refuse
>   To drink. O fearful sin !

"The council, which is thought most wise,
   Did sit so long upon it,
That they grew weary and did rise,
   And could make nothing on it."

According to a letter of Chamberlain to Carleton, indexed among the *State Papers*, the Tityres were a secret society first formed in Lord Vaux's regiment in the Low Countries, and their "prince" was called Ottoman. Another entry shows that the "Bugle" mentioned by Yonge was the badge of a society originally distinct from the Tityres, which afterwards joined with it. The date of Herrick's poem is thus fixed as December, 162¾, and this is confirmed by another sentence in the same passage in *Yonge's Diary*, in which he says: "The Jesuits and Papists do wonderfully swarm in the city, and rumours lately have been given out for firing the Navy and House of Munition, on which are set a double guard". The Parliament to which Herrick alludes was actually summoned in January, 1624, to meet on February 12. Sir Simeon Steward, to whom the poem is addressed, was of the family of the Stewards of Stantney, in the Isle of Ely. He was knighted with his father, Mark Steward, in 1603, and afterwards became a fellow-commoner of Trinity Hall, Cambridge. He was at different times Sheriff and Deputy-Lieutenant for Cambridgeshire, and while serving in the latter capacity got into some trouble for unlawful exactions. In 1627 he wrote a poem on the *King of the Fairies Clothes* in the same vein as Herrick's fairy pieces.

321. *Then is the work half done.* As Dr. Grosart suggests, Herrick may have had in mind the "Dimidium facti qui cœpit habet" of Horace, I. *Epist.* ii. 40. But here the emphasis is on beginning *well*, there on *beginning*.

Begin with Jove is doubtless from the "Ab Jove principium, Musæ," of Virg. *Ecl.* iii. 60.

323. *Fears not the fierce sedition of the seas.* A reminiscence of Horace, III. *Od.* i. 25-32.

328. *Gold before goodness.* Printed in *Witts Recreations*, 1650, as *A Foolish Querie.* The sentiment is from Seneca, *Ep.* cxv.: An dives, omnes quærimus ; nemo, an bonus. Cp. Juvenal, III. 140 sqq.; Plaut. *Menæchm.* IV. ii. 6.

331. *To his honoured kinsman, Sir William Soame.* The second son of Sir Stephen Soame, Lord Mayor of London in 1598. Herrick's father and Sir Stephen married sisters.

As benjamin and storax when they meet. Instances of the use of "Benjamin" for gum benzoin will be found in the Dictionaries. Dr. Grosart's gloss, "*Benjamin*, the favourite youngest son of the Patriarch," is unfortunate.

336. *His Age: dedicated to . . . M. John Wickes under the name of Posthumus.* There is an important version of this poem in Egerton MS., 2725, where it is entitled *Mr. Herrick's Old Age to Mr. Weekes.* I do not think it has been collated before. Stanzas i.-vi. contain few variants; ii. 6 reads: "Dislikes to care for what's behind"; iii. 6: "Like a lost maidenhead," for "Like to a lily lost"; v. 8: "With the best and whitest stone"; vi. 1: "We'll

not be poor". After this we have two stanzas
omitted in 1648 :—

> "We have no vineyards which do bear
>   Their lustful clusters all the year,
>   Nor odoriferous
>   Orchards, like to Alcinous ;
>   Nor gall the seas
>   Our witty appetites to please
>   With mullet, turbot, gilt-head bought
>   At a high rate and further brought.

> "Nor can we glory of a great
>   And stuffed magazine of wheat ;
>   We have no bath
>   Of oil, but only rich in faith
>   O'er which the hand
>   Of fortune can have no command,
>   But what she gives not, she not takes,
>   But of her own a spoil she makes."

Stanza vii., l. 2, has "close" for "both"; l. 3
"see" for "have"; l. 6, "open" for "that cheap";
l. 7, "full" for "same". Stanzas x.-xvii. have so
many variants that I am obliged to transcribe them
in full, though they show Herrick not at his best,
and the poem is not one to linger over :—

10.

> "Live in thy peace; as for myself,
>   When I am bruisèd on the shelf
>   Of Time, and *read*

Eternal daylight o'er my head :
 When with the rheum,
With cough *and* ptisick, I consume
Into an heap of cinders ; then
The Ages fled I'll call again,

11.

" And with a tear compare these last
 And cold times unto those are past,
  While Baucis by
With her lean lips shall kiss *them dry*
  Then will we sit
By the fire, foretelling snow and sleet
And weather by our aches, grown
†Old enough to be our own

12.

" True Calendar [   ]
 Is for to know what change is near,
  Then to assuage
The gripings *in* the chine by age,
  I'll call my young
Iülus to sing such a song
I made upon my *mistress'* breast ;
Or such a blush at such a feast.

13.

" Then shall he read *my Lily fine*
 Entomb'd within a crystal shrine :
  My Primrose next :
A piece then of a higher text ;
  For to beget

In me a more transcendent heat
Than that insinuating fire
Which crept into each *reverend* Sire,

14.

" When the *high* Helen *her fair cheeks*
Showed to the army of the Greeks ;
     At which I'll *rise*
(Blind though as midnight in my eyes),
     And hearing it,
Flutter and crow, *and*, in a fit
Of *young* concupiscence, and *feel*
New flames within the aged steal.

15.

" Thus frantic, crazy man (God wot),
I'll call to mind *the times* forgot
     And oft between
Sigh out the Times that *we* have seen !
     And shed a tear,
And twisting my Iülus *hair,*
Doting, I'll weep and say (in truth)
Baucis, these were *the* sins of youth.

16.

" Then *will I* cause my hopeful Lad
(If a wild Apple can be had)
     To crown the Hearth
(Lar thus conspiring with our mirth) ;
     Next to infuse
Our *better beer* into the cruse :
Which, neatly spiced, we'll first carouse
Unto the *Vesta* of the house.

17.

" Then the next health to friends of mine
In oysters, and Burgundian wine,
Hind, Goderiske, Smith,
And Nansagge, sons of *clune* and* pith,
Such *who know* well
To board the magic *bowl,* and *spill*
All mighty blood, and can do more
Than Jove and Chaos them before."

This John Wickes or Weekes is spoken of by
Anthony à Wood as a "jocular person " and a popular
preacher.   He enters Wood's *Fasti* by right of his
co-optation as a D.D. in 1643, while the court was
at Oxford; his education had been at Cambridge.
He was a prebendary of Bristol and Dean of St. Burian
in Cornwall, and suffered some persecution as a
royalist.   Herrick later on, when himself shedless
and cottageless, addresses another poem to him as
his "peculiar friend,"

To whose glad threshold and free door
I may, a poet, come, though poor.

A friend suggests that Hind may have been John
Hind, an Anacreontic poet and friend of Greene,
and has found references to a Thomas Goodricke
of St. John's Coll., Camb., author of two poems
on the accession of James I., and a Martin
Nansogge, B.A. of Trinity Hall, 1614, afterwards
vicar of Cornwood, Devon.   Smith is certainly

---

* Clune = "clunis," a haunch.

20

James Smith, who, with Sir John Mennis, edited
the *Musarum Deliciæ*, in which the first poem
is addressed "to Parson Weekes: an invitation
to London," and contains a reference to—

"That old sack
Young Herrick took to entertain
The Muses in a sprightly vein".

The early part of this poem contains, along with
the name Posthumus, many Horatian reminiscences:
cp. especially II. *Od.* xiv. 1-8, and IV. *Od.* vii. 14.
It may be noted that in the imitation of the latter
passage in stanza iv. the MS. copy at the Museum
corrects the misplacement of the epithet, reading :—

"But we must on and thither tend
Where Tullus and rich Ancus blend," etc.,

for "Where Ancus and rich Tullus".

Again the variant, "*Open* candle baudery," in verse
7, is an additional argument against Dr. Grosart's
explanation: "Obscene words and figures made
with candle-smoke," the allusion being merely to the
blackened ceilings produced by cheap candles without a shade.

337. *A Short Hymn to Venus.* Printed in *Witts
Recreations*, 1650, as *A vow to Cupid*, with variants:
l. 1, *Cupid* for *Goddess ;* l. 2, *like* for *with ;* l. 3,
that I may for *I may but ;* l. 5, *do* for *will.*

340. *Upon a delaying lady.* Printed in *Witts
Recreations*, 1650, as *A Check to her delay.*

341. *The Lady Mary Villars*, niece of the first
Duke of Buckingham, married successively Charles,
son of Philip, Earl of Pembroke, Esme Stuart, Duke

of Richmond and Lennox, and Thomas Howard.
Died 1685.

355. *Hath filed upon my silver hairs.* Cp. Ben
Jonson, *The King's Entertainment* :—

"What all the minutes, hours, weeks, months, and
    years
That hang in file upon these silver hairs
Could not produce," etc.

359. *Philip, Earl of Pembroke and Montgomery.*
Philip Herbert (born 1584, died 1650), despite his
foul mouth, ill temper, and devotion to sport ("He
would make an excellent chancellor to the mews
were Oxford turned into a kennel of hounds," wrote
the author of *Mercurius Menippeus* when Pembroke
succeeded Laud as chancellor), was also a patron of
literature. He was one of the "incomparable pair of
brethren" to whom the Shakespeare folio of 1623 was
dedicated, and he was a good friend to Massinger.
His fondness for scribbling in the margins of books
may, or may not, be considered as further evidence
of a respect for literature.

366. *Thou shalt not all die.* Horace's "non omnis
moriar".

367. *Upon Wrinkles.* Printed in *Witts Recreations*, 1650, under the title *To a Stale Lady*. The
first line there reads :—

    " Thy wrinkles are no more nor less".

375. *Anne Soame, now Lady Abdie,* eldest daughter
of Sir Thomas Soame, and second wife of Sir Thomas
Abdy, Bart., of Felix Hall, Essex. Herrick's poem
is modelled on Mart. III. lxv.

376. *Upon his Kinswoman, Mistress Elizabeth Herrick*, daughter of the poet's brother Nicholas.

377. *A Panegyric to Sir Lewis Pemberton* of Rushden, in Northamptonshire, sheriff of the county in 1622; married Alice, daughter of Tho. Bowles. Died 1641. With this poem cp. Ben Jonson's *Epig.* ci.

But great and large she spreads by dust and sweat. Dr. Grosart very appositely quotes Montaigne: "For it seemeth that the verie name of vertue presupposeth difficultie and inferreth resistance, and cannot well exercise it selfe without an enemie" (Florio's tr., p. 233). But I think the two passages have a common origin in some version of Hesiod's τῆς ἀρετῆς ἱδρῶτα θεοὶ προπάροιθεν ἔθηκαν, which is twice quoted by Plato.

382. *After the rare arch-poet, Jonson, died.* Perhaps suggested by the Epitaph of Plautus on himself, *ap.* Gell. i. 24:—

Postquam est mortem aptus Plautus, comoedia
　　luget;
Scena deserta, dein risus, ludu' jocusque,
Et numeri innumeri simul omnes collacruma-
　　runt.

384. *To his nephew, to be prosperous in painting.* This artistic nephew may have been a Wingfield, son of Mercy Herrick, who married John Wingfield, of Brantham, Suffolk; or one of three sons of Nicholas Herrick and Susanna Salter, or Thomas, or some unknown son of Thomas Herrick. There is no record of any painter Herrick's achievements.

392. *Sir Edward Fish, Knight Baronet*, of Chertsey, in Surrey. Died 1658.

405. *Nor fear or spice or fish.* Herrick is remembering Persius, i. 43: Nec scombros metuentia carmina, nec thus. To form the paper jacket or *tunica* which wrapt the mackerel in Roman cookery seems to have been the ultimate employment of many poems. Cp. Mart. III. l. 9; IV. lxxxvii. 8; and Catullus, XCV. 8.

The farting Tanner and familiar King. The ballad here alluded to is that of *King Edward IV. and the tanner of Tamworth*, printed in Prof. Child's collection. " The dancing friar tattered in the bush " of the next line is one of the heroes of the old ballad of *The Fryar and the Boye*, printed by Wynkyn de Worde, and included in the Appendix to Furnivall and Hales' edition of the Percy folio. The boy was the possessor of a "magic flute," and, having got the friar into a bush, made him dance there.

> " Jack, as he piped, laughed among,
>   The Friar with briars was vilely stung,
>   He hopped wondrous high.
>   At last the Friar held up his hand
>   And said: I can no longer stand,
>   Oh! I shall dancing die."

" Those monstrous lies of little Robin Rush " is explained by Dr. Grosart as an allusion to " The Historie of Friar Rush, how he came to a House of Religion to seek a Service, and being entertained by the Prior was made First Cook, being full of pleasant Mirth and Delight for young people ". Of " Tom

Chipperfield and pretty lisping Ned" I can find nothing. "The flying Pilchard and the frisking Dace" probably belong to the fish monsters alluded to in the *Tempest.* In "Tim Trundell" Herrick seems for the sake of alliteration to have taken a liberty with the Christian name of a well-known ballad publisher.

He's greedy of his life. From Seneca, *Thyestes,* 884-85 :—

> Vitæ est avidus quisquis non vult
> Mundo secum pereunte mori.

407. *Upon Himself.* 408. *Another.* Both printed in *Witts Recreations,* 1650, the second under the title of *Love and Liberty.* This last is taken from Corn. Gall. *Eleg.* i. 6, quoted by Montaigne, iii. 5 :—

> Et mihi dulce magis resoluto vivere collo.

412. *The Mad Maid's Song.* A manuscript version of this song is contained in Harleian MS. 6917, fol. 48, ver. 80. The chief variants are : st. i. l. 2, *morrow* for *morning ;* l. 4, *all dabbled* for *bedabbled ;* st. ii. l. 1, *cowslip* for *primrose ;* l. 3, *tears* for *flowers ;* l. 4, *was* for *is ;* st. v. l. 1, *hope* for *know ;* st. vii. l. 2, *balsam* for *cowslips.*

415. *Whither dost thou whorry me.* Quo me, Bacche, rapis tui Plenum ? Hor. III. *Od.* xxv. 1.

430. *As Sallust saith, i.e.,* the pseudo-Sallust in the *Epist. ad Cai. Cæs. de Repub. Ordinanda.*

431. *Every time seems short.* Epigr. in Farnabii, *Florileg.* [a. 1629] :—

> Τοῖσι μὲν εὖ πράττουσιν ἅπας ὁ βίος βραχύς ἐστιν·
> Τοῖς δὲ κακῶς, μία νὺξ ἄπλετός ἐστι χρόνος.

443. *Oberon's Palace.—After the feast (my Shap-cott) see.* See 223, 293, from which it is a pity that this poem should have been divorced. Of the *Palace* there are as many as three MS. versions, viz., Add. 22, 603 (p. 59), and Add. 25, 303 (p. 157), at the British Museum, both of which I have collated, and Ashmole MS. 38, which I only know through my predecessors. The three MSS. appear to agree very harmoniously, and they unite in increasing our knowledge of Herrick by a passage of twenty-seven lines, following on the words "And here and there and farther off," and in lieu of the next four and a half lines in *Hesperides.* They read as follows:—

" Some sort of pear,
Apple or plum, is neatly laid
(As if it was a tribute paid)
By the round urchin ; some mixt wheat
The which the ant did taste, not eat ;
Deaf nuts, soft Jews'-ears, and some thin
Chippings, the mice filched from the bin
Of the gray farmer, and to these
The scraps of lentils, chitted peas,
Dried honeycombs, brown acorn cups,
Out of the which he sometimes sups
His herby broth, and there close by
Are pucker'd bullace, cankers (?), dry
Kernels, and withered haws ; the rest
Are trinkets fal'n from the kite's nest,
As butter'd bread, the which the wild
Bird snatched away from the crying child,
Blue pins, tags, fesenes, beads and things
Of higher price, as half-jet rings,

Ribbons and then some silken shreaks
The virgins lost at barley-breaks.
Many a purse-string, many a thread
Of gold and silver therein spread,
Many a counter, many a die,
Half rotten and without an eye,
Lies here about, and, as we guess,
Some bits of thimbles seem to dress
The brave cheap work; *and for to pave*
The excellency of this cave,
Squirrels and children's teeth late shed,
Serve here, both which *enchequered*
With castors' doucets, which poor they
Bite off themselves to 'scape away:
Brown *toadstones,* ferrets' eyes, *the gum*
That shines," etc.

The italicised words in the last few lines appear
in *Hesperides;* all the rest are new.   Other variants
are: "The grass of Lemster ore soberly sparkling"
for "the finest Lemster ore mildly disparkling";
"girdle" for "ceston"; "The eyes of all doth
strait bewitch" for "All with temptation doth bewitch"; "choicely hung" for "neatly hung";
"silver roach" for "silvery fish"; "cave" for
"room"; "get reflection" for "make reflected";
"Candlemas" for "taper-light"; "moon-tane" for
"moon-tanned," etc., etc.

Kings though they're hated.   The "Oderint dum
metuant" of the *Atreus* of Accius, quoted by Cicero
and Seneca.

446. *To Oenone.*   Printed in *Witts Recreations,*

1650, under the title: " The Farewell to Love and
to his Mistress," and with the unlucky misprint
" court" for " covet " (also " for" for " but ") in the
stanza iii. l. 1.

447. *Grief breaks the stoutest heart.* Frangit
fortia corda dolor. Tibull. III. ii. 6.

451. *To the right gracious Prince, Lodowick, Duke
of Richmond and Lennox.* There appears to me to
be a blunder here which Dr. Grosart and Mr. Hazlitt
do not elucidate, by recording the birth of Lodowick, first Duke of Richmond, in 1574, his succession
to the Lennox title in 1583, creation as Duke of
Richmond in May, 1623, and death in the following
February. For this first duke was no " stem " left
" of all those three brave brothers fallen in the war,"
and the allusion here is undoubtedly to his nephews—
George, Lord d'Aubigny, who fell at Edgehill; Lord
John Stewart, who fell at Alresford; and Lord Bernard Stewart (Earl of Lichfield), who fell at Rowton
Heath. In elucidation of Herrick's Dirge (219) over
the last of these three brothers, I have already
quoted Clarendon's remark, that he was " the third
brother of that illustrious family that sacrificed his
life in this quarrel," and it cannot be doubted that
Herrick is here alluding to the same fact. The
poem must therefore have been written after 1645,
i.e., more than twenty years after the death of Duke
Lodowick. But the duke then living was James,
who succeeded his father Esme in 1624, was re-
created Duke of Richmond in 1641, and did not die
till 1655. It is true that there was a brother named
Lodovic, but he was an abbot in France and never

succeeded to the title.   Herrick, therefore, seems to
have blundered in the Christian name.

453. *Let's live in haste.*   From Martial, VII. xlvii.
11, 12:—

> Vive velut rapto : fugitivaque gaudia carpe :
> Perdiderit nullum vita reversa diem.

457. *While Fates permit.* From Seneca, *Herc. Fur.*
177 :—

> Dum Fata sinunt,
> Vivite laeti : properat cursu
> Vita citato, volucrique die
> Rota praecipitis vertitur anni.

459. *With Horace* (IV. *Od.* ix. 29) :—

> Paulùm sepultae distat inertiae
> Celata virtus.

465. *The parting Verse or charge to his Supposed
Wife when he travelled.*   MS. variants of this poem
are found at the British Museum in Add. 22, 603,
and in Ashmole MS. 38.   Their title, " Mr. Herrick's
charge to his wife," led Mr. Payne Collier to rashly
identify with the poet a certain Robert Herrick
married at St. Clement Danes, 1632, to a Jane
Gibbons.   The variants are numerous, but not very
important.   In l. 4 we have " draw wooers " for
" draw thousands"; ll. 11-16 are transposed to after
l. 28 ; and "Are the expressions of that itch " is
written " As emblems will express that itch "; ll. 27,
28 appear as :—

> " For that once lost thou *needst must fall*
> *To one, then prostitute to all :*

And we then have the transposed passage :—

Nor so immurèd would I have
Thee live, as dead, *or* in thy grave;
But walk abroad, yet wisely well
Keep 'gainst my coming sentinel,
And think *each man thou seest doth doom
Thy thoughts to say, I back am come.*

Farther on we have the rather pretty variant:—

    " Let them *call thee wondrous fair,
      Crown of women,* yet despair ".

Eight lines lower "virtuous" is read for "gentle,"
and the omission of some small words throws some
light on a change in Herrick's metrical views as he
grew older. The words omitted are bracketed:—

    "[And] Let thy dreams be only fed
    With this, that I am in thy bed.
    And [thou] then turning in that sphere,
    Waking findst [shall find] me sleeping there.
    But [yet] if boundless lust must scale
    Thy fortress and *must* needs prevail
    'Gainst thee and force a passage in," etc.

Other variants are: " Creates the action " for "That
makes the action"; "Glory" for "Triumph";
" my last signet" for "this compression"; "turn
again in my full triumph" for "come again, As
one triumphant," and "the height of womankind"
for " all faith of womankind ".

The body sins not, 'tis the will, etc. A maxim of
law Latin: Actus non facit reum nisi mens sit rea.

466. *To his Kinsman, Sir Thos. Soame,* son of
Sir Stephen Soame, Lord Mayor of London, 1589,
and of Anne Stone, Herrick's aunt. Sir Thomas

was Sheriff of London, 1635, M.P. for the City,
1640, and died Jan., 1670. See Cussan's *Hertfort-
shire.* (*Hundred of Edwinstree*, p. 100.)

470. *Few Fortunate.* A variant on the text (Matt.
xx. 16): " Many be called but few chosen ".

479. *To Rosemary and Bays.* The use of rosemary and bays at weddings forms a section in Brand's
chapter on marriage customs (ii. 119). For the
gilding he quotes from a wedding sermon preached
in 1607 by Roger Hacket: " Smell sweet, O ye
owers, in your native sweetness : be not gilded
with the idle art of man ". The use of gloves at
weddings forms the subject of another section in
Brand (ii. 125). He "quotes Ben Jonson's *Silent
Woman :* " We see no ensigns of a wedding here, no
character of a bridal ; where be our scarves and our
gloves ? "

483. *To his worthy friend, M. Thomas Falcon-
brige.* As Herrick hints at his friend's destiny for
a public career, it seemed worth while to hunt
through the Calendar of State Papers for a chance
reference to this Falconbridge, who so far has
evaded editors. He is apparently the Mr. Thomas
Falconbridge (who appears in various papers between 1640 and 1644, as passing accounts, and in
the latter year was " Receiver-General at Westminster ".

Towers reared high, etc. Cp. Horace, *Od.* II. x.
9-12.

> Saepius ventis agitatur ingens
> Pinus, et celsae graviore casu
> Decidunt turres, feriuntque summos
> Fulgura montes.

486. *He's lord of thy life*, etc. Seneca, *Epist. Mor.* iv.: Quisquis vitam suam contempsit tuae dominus est. Quoted by Montaigne, I. xxiii.

488. *Shame is a bad attendant to a state.* From Seneca, *Hippol.* 431 : Malus est minister regii imperii pudor.

He rents his crown that fears the people's hate. Also from Seneca, *Oedipus*, 701 : Odia qui nimium timet regnare nescit.

496. *To his honoured kinsman, Sir Richard Stone,* son of John Stone, sergeant-at-law, the brother of Julian Stone, Herrick's mother. He died in 1660.

To this white temple of my heroes. Ben Jonson's admirers were proud to call themselves "sealed of the tribe of Ben," and Herrick, a devout Jonsonite, seems to have imitated the idea so far as to plan sometimes, as here, a Temple, sometimes a Book (see *infra*, 512), sometimes a City (365), a Plantation (392), a Calendar (545), a College (983), of his own favourite friends, to whom his poetry was to give immortality. The earliest direct reference to this plan is in his address to John Selden, the antiquary (365), in which he writes :—

" A city here of heroes I have made
   Upon the rock whose firm foundation laid
   Shall never shrink ; where, making thine abode,
   Live thou a Selden, that's a demi-god ".

It is noteworthy that the poems which contain the clearest reference to this Temple (or its variants) are mostly addressed to kinsfolk, *e.g.*, this to Sir Richard Stone, to Mrs. Penelope Wheeler, to Mr. Stephen

Soame, and to Susanna and Thomas Herrick. Other recipients of the honour are Sir Edward Fish and Dr. Alabaster, Jack Crofts, Master J. Jincks, etc.

497. *All flowers sent, etc.* See Virgil's—or the Virgilian—*Culex*, ll. 397-410.

Martial's bee. See *Epig.* IV. xxxii.

De ape electro inclusa.
Et latet et lucet Phaethontide condita gutta,
　Ut videatur apis nectare clausa suo.
Dignum tantorum pretium tulit illa laborum.
　Credibile est ipsam sic voluisse mori.

500. *To Mistress Dorothy Parsons.* This "saint" from Herrick's Temple may certainly be identified with the second of the three children (William, Dorothy, and Thomasine) of Mr. John Parsons, organist and master of the choristers at Westminster Abbey, where he was buried in 1623. Herrick addresses another poem to her sister Thomasine :—

"Grow up in beauty, as thou dost begin,
　And be of all admired, Thomasine ".

502. *'Tis sin to throttle wine.* Martial, I. xix. 5 : Scelus est jugulare Falernum.

506. *Edward, Earl of Dorset,* Knight of the Garter, grandson of Thomas Sackville, author of *Gorboduc.* He succeeded his brother, Richard Sackville, the third earl, in 1624, and died in 1652. Clarendon describes a duel which he fought with Lord Bruce in Flanders.

Of your own self a public theatre. Cp. Burton (Democ. to Reader) "Ipse mihi theatrum ".

510. *To his Kinswoman, Mrs. Penelope Wheeler.* See Note on 130.

511. *A mighty strife 'twixt form and chastity.* Lis est cum formâ magna pudicitiæ. Quoted from Ovid by Burton, who translates: " Beauty and honesty have ever been at odds ".

514. *To the Lady Crew, upon the death of her child.* This must be the child buried in Westminster Abbey, according to the entry in the register " 163⅞, Feb. 6. ' Sir Clipsy Crewe's daughter, in the North aisle of the monuments." Colonel Chester annotates : " She was a younger daughter, and was born at Crewe, 27th July, 1631. She died on the 4th of February, and must have been an independent heiress, as her father administered to her estate on the 24th May following."

515. *Here needs no Court for our Request.* An allusion to the Court of Requests, established in the time of Richard II. as a lesser Court of Equity for the hearing of "all poor men's suits ". It was abolished in 1641, at the same time as the Star Chamber.

517. *The new successor drives away old love.* From Ovid, *Rem. Am.* 462 : Successore novo vincitur omnis amor.

519. *Born I was to meet with age.* Cp. 540. From Anacreon, 38 [24] :—

ʼΕπείδη βρότος ἐτέχθην,
Βιότου τρίβον ὁδεύειν,
Χρόνον ἔγνων ὃν παρῆλθον,
ʼʹΟν δʼ ἔχω δραμεῖν οὐκ οἶδα·

Μέθετέ με, φροντίδες ·
Μηδέν μοι καὶ ὑμῖν ἔστω.
Πρὶν ἐμὲ φθάσῃ τὸ τέρμα,
Παίξω, γελάσω, χορεύσω,
Μετὰ τοῦ καλοῦ Λυαίου.

520. *Fortune did never favour one.* From Dionys. Halicarn., as quoted by Burton, II. iii. 1, § 1.

521. *To Phillis to love and live with him.* A variant on Marlowe's theme : "Come live with me and be my love". Donne's *The Bait* (printed in Grosart's edition, vol. ii. p. 206) is another.

522. *To his Kinswoman, Mistress Susanna Herrick,* wife of his elder brother Nicholas.

523. *Susanna Southwell.* Probably a daughter of Sir Thomas Southwell, for whom Herrick wrote the Epithalamium (No. 149).

525. *Her pretty feet,* etc. Cp. Suckling's "Ballad upon a Wedding":—

> " Her feet beneath her petticoat,
>   Like little mice stole in and out,
>   As if they feared the light ".

526. *To his Honoured Friend, Sir John Mynts.* John Mennis, a Vice-Admiral of the fleet and knighted in 1641, refused to join in the desertion of the fleet to the Parliament. After the Restoration he was made Governor of Dover and Chief Comptroller of the Navy. He was one of the editors of the collection called *Musarum Deliciæ* (1656), in the first poem of which there is an allusion to—

" That old sack
Young Herrick took to entertain
The Muses in a sprightly vein ".

527. *Fly me not*, etc. From Anacreon, 49 [34]:—

Μή με φύγῃς, ὁρῶσα
Τὰν πολιὰν ἔθειραν · . . .
Ὄρα κἂν στεφάνοισιν
Ὄπως πρέπει τὰ λευκὰ
Ῥόδοις κρίν' ἐμπλακέντα.

529. *As thou deserv'st be proud.* Cp. Hor. III.
Od. xxx. 14 :—

Sume superbiam
Quaesitam meritis et mihi Delphica
Lauro cinge volens, Melpomene, comam.

534. *To Electra.* Printed in *Witts Recreations*,
1650, where it is entitled *To Julia.*

536. *Ill Government.* . . . *When kings obey*, etc.
From Seneca, *Octav.* 581 :—

Male imperatur, cum regit vulgus duces.

545. *To his Worthy Kinsman, Mr. Stephen Soame*
(the son or, less probably, the brother of Sir Thomas
Soame) : *One of my righteous tribe.* Cp. Note to
498.

547. *Great spirits never with their bodies die.*
Tacit. *Agric.* 46 :—" Si quis piorum manibus locus,
si, ut sapientibus placet, non cum corpore extingu-
untur magnae animae ".

554. *Die thou canst not all.* Hor. IV. *Od.* xxx.
6, 7.

556. *The Fairies.* Cp. the old ballad of *Robin Goodfellow* :—

> "When house or hearth doth sluttish lie,
>   I pinch the maids both black and blue " ;

and Ben Jonson's *Entertainment at Althorpe*, etc.

557. *M. John Weare, Councellour.* Probably the same as " the much-lamented Mr. J. Warr " of 134.

Law is to give to every one his own. Cicero, *De Fin.* v. : Animi affectio suum cuique tribuens Justitia dicitur.

562. *His Kinswoman, Bridget Herrick*, eldest daughter of his brother Nicholas.

563. *The Wanton Satyr.* See Sir E. Dyer's *The Shepherd's Conceit of Prometheus* :—

> " Prometheus, when first from heaven high
>   He brought down fire, ere then on earth not seen,
>   Fond of delight, a Satyr standing by
>   Gave it a kiss, as it like sweet had been.
>
>   .   .   .   .
>
>   The difference is—the Satyr's lips, my heart,
>   He for a time, I evermore, have smart."

So *Euphues :* " Satirus not knowing what fire was would needs embrace it and was burnt; " and Sir John Davies, *False and True Knowledge.*